GRE®

FOR DUMMIES®

A Wiley Brand

Quick Prep Edition

Quick Prep Edition

by Ron Woldoff, MBA, MIS
Founder, National Test Prep

with Joe Kraynak

GRE® For Dummies®, Quick Prep Edition

Published by
John Wiley & Sons, Inc.
111 River Street
Hoboken, NJ 07030-5774
www.wiley.com

Contents at a Glance

Table of Contents

Introduction

Welcome to *GRE For Dummies*, Quick Prep Edition. Don't take the dummies thing personally — you're obviously no dummy. You made it through high school with high enough grades and test scores to get into college. You then graduated to join the elite group of approximately 30 percent of U.S. citizens who hold bachelor's degrees, and some of you already have advanced degrees. And now you're ready to go further.

Between you and your goal is the GRE: a test designed solely to challenge your ability to remember everything you've forgotten since high school — material you haven't touched in years. Maybe you feel confident that you know your stuff and don't need to review right triangles, prefixes and suffixes, and tips on finding the main idea in a reading passage. If that's the case, you've come to the right place.

This book gives you an overview of the GRE in order to successfully reach your goal: admittance to the grad school of your choice and perhaps a scholarship to help pay your way. In your hands is a concise guide to the GRE that includes two practice exams to help you get comfortable with the test format and get familiar with the various content you'll likely encounter on the exam. If you need a fast, effective introduction to the GRE, you're holding the right book.

About This Book

In *GRE For Dummies,* Quick Prep Edition, I introduce you to the GRE, offer some test-taking strategies, and then present two practice exams that you can use to gauge how you'll do on the test when it counts. After you take a practice exam, be sure to review the answer explanation for *every* question. If you don't have time for in-depth studying, looking at the answer explanations may be enough of a refresher to help you bump up your score on the GRE by a point or two.

Foolish Assumptions

This book is intended to help you prepare for the GRE. I assume that you're in at least one of these three stages of your GRE planning:

✔ You've already scheduled the GRE, or are about to, and you want to sharpen your test-taking skills in preparation for the exam.

✔ You have to take the GRE for acceptance into the graduate program at your preferred school.

✔ You're considering a graduate program or school that requires the GRE as part of the application process and want to know what the exam is all about and see how you'd perform on the exam.

Icons Used in This Book

Although everything included in this book is valuable, some tidbits call for special attention. Look for the following icons to quickly spot the most important information.

This icon indicates little bits of wisdom to make your GRE experience go more smoothly and improve your success.

This icon marks key points to remember while you're taking the GRE, especially anything that's likely to surprise you on the test. By knowing what to expect, you're better prepared to handle it.

Where to Go from Here

If you've already signed up to take the GRE, you may want to jump right to one of the practice exams to see how well you do in a mock testing situation. After you take the test, be sure to review the answer explanations for all the questions — not just the ones you answered incorrectly. Reviewing all the explanations will reinforce what you already know, and you never know, but you may just pick up a new fact or two.

If the GRE remains a big mystery to you but you know you need to take it to get into grad school, start with Chapter 1 to get the lowdown on the exam. Then keep reading to get some advice about studying for the exam and preparing for test day.

If after taking the practice exams in Part II, you think you could benefit from some additional review in a particular area, I encourage you to pick up the latest edition of *GRE For Dummies*. That book includes detailed reviews of the various content that makes up the Verbal and Quantitative Reasoning sections of the exam; it also includes additional practice tests.

Part I
Getting Started with the GRE

In this part . . .

✔ Get the details about signing up for the GRE, what's on the exam, and how your score is calculated.

✔ Figure out how to schedule your study time in advance of test day and get some pointers if you're retaking the exam.

✔ Know what you need to do to prepare for the exam (beyond studying) and find out what to expect on test day.

Chapter 1

Knowing What to Expect with the GRE

. . . .

In This Chapter

▶ Fitting the GRE into your schedule

▶ Deconstructing the GRE to better understand what's on it

▶ Grasping the scoring system

▶ Looking forward to intermissions

. . . .

*O*ne of the easiest ways to reduce your test anxiety and optimize your performance on the GRE is to become familiar with it. Knowing what to expect gives you less to think about and fret over come test day so you can focus on what really matters — the test itself.

In this chapter, I encourage you to schedule your exam early so you can get a time slot that works for you. I also discuss the GRE's structure and scoring system so you can build your strategies around them. With this guidance, you're better equipped to avoid surprises that may throw you off your game.

Signing Up for the GRE

In most parts of the world, the GRE is a computer-based test, which makes it easier to administer to individual test-takers. Sign up early so you can choose the day, time, and place that work best for you. If you're a morning person who's sharpest at sunrise, you can schedule the test for early morning; if you're a night owl who tends to sleep in, you can opt for late morning or early afternoon. Actual time slot availability varies according to the testing center, but you have more days and times to choose from than you do with paper-and-pencil tests, such as the LSAT and SAT.

The paper and computer versions of the GRE are slightly different. For example, the paper version has 25 questions per section, while the computer version has only 20. Don't worry too much about the differences; your only option will most likely be to take the computer version.

To sign up for the GRE, see the current *GRE Information and Registration Bulletin* (available through most college admissions offices), register online at www.ets.org, or register via phone by calling 800-473-2255. You can also check the GRE testing center locations and available time slots at www.ets.org.

To help you get in the right mindset, take the practice tests at the same time of day you plan on taking the real thing. (Check out the practice tests in Chapters 4 and 6.) I've had students use this strategy to become accustomed to the effects that their *circadian rhythms* (hunger and nap patterns) have on their test-taking abilities. If you're used to eating or relaxing at a certain time each day, make sure these tendencies don't sneak up on you during the exam. One of your goals is to make the GRE as familiar as possible, or rather, to make the test-taking experience as less *un*familiar as possible. (See Chapter 3 for more on how to prepare for the GRE.)

Because the computerized GRE is administered to individual test-takers, testing centers tend to have few seats, and those seats fill up quickly during peak admission deadline months (April and November). If you're planning to take the GRE around these months (to get your test scores in on time), schedule your test early and secure your ideal time slot. You can always reschedule, but the last thing you need is an inconvenient time or location. One of my students waited until the last minute to schedule his exam, and he had to drive from Phoenix to Tucson (approximately 120 miles) to take his GRE and get his scores in on time. He called me during his drive to review math formulas, but this wasn't an ideal way to ramp up for the test.

Breaking the GRE into Manageable Pieces

Standardized tests tend to convey a sense of gloom and doom. Telling someone you have to take the SAT, ACT, or GRE usually elicits the same facial expression as saying that you need to have your wisdom teeth pulled. However, breaking the GRE down into its component parts makes it more manageable and less threatening.

Table 1-1 provides a quick overview of what's on the exam. The essays are always first, but the multiple-choice sections may be in any order.

Table 1-1	GRE Breakdown by Section (Computer-Based)	
Section	*Number of Questions*	*Time Allotted*
Analyze an Issue	1 essay	30 minutes
Analyze an Argument	1 essay	30 minutes
Verbal Section	20 questions	30 minutes
Math (Quantitative) Section	20 questions	35 minutes
Verbal Section	20 questions	30 minutes
Math (Quantitative) Section	20 questions	35 minutes
Discreetly Unscored Math or Verbal Section (may be earlier in the exam)	20 questions	30 or 35 minutes

At close to four hours long, the GRE challenges your stamina as much as your ability to answer the questions. No matter how solid your math and verbal skills are, you must maintain the concentration and focus needed to do well for four hours, which isn't easy on a challenging task such as the GRE. You can build your test-taking stamina by practicing in four-hour stretches and taking multiple timed practice tests.

The GRE includes one unscored Math or Verbal section in addition to the scored sections. So you actually have three Math *or* three Verbal sections, with one of those sections unscored. This unscored section neither helps nor hurts your score. The GRE may indicate that the section is unscored, but usually it doesn't, so be sure to work all of the sections to the best of your ability.

Unlike other computer-based tests (such as the GMAT and TOEFL), the GRE allows you to skip questions and return to them later, as long as you're still in the section. When you reach the end of a section, the GRE displays a review screen that indicates any unanswered questions. If you have time remaining in the section, return to these questions and answer them as well as you can. This feature is nice because you can knock out all the easy questions before spending time on the hard ones. (See Chapter 2 for tips on managing your time during the exam.)

In each section, the questions are worth the same number of points, and within that section, they don't become more or less difficult based on your performance. However, on the computer version of the exam, your performance on the Math or Verbal section determines the overall difficulty level of the *next* Math or Verbal section. For example, if you do extremely well on the first Math section, the GRE makes the second Math section harder. Even if you don't get many questions right in the second Math section, your score may be higher than the score of someone who answers more easier questions correctly, because GRE scoring accommodates for the difficulty level of the questions.

So exactly what types of questions and how many of each type can you expect to run into on the GRE? Check out Table 1-2 for the answers.

Table 1-2	GRE Breakdown by Question Type
Type of Question	*Approximate Number of Questions*
Per Math Section (20 questions each)	
Multiple-choice with exactly one correct answer	6
Multiple-choice with one or more correct answers	2
Fill-in-the-blank with the correct answer	2
Data Interpretation (based on graphs)	3
Quantitative Comparisons	7
Per Verbal Section (20 questions each)	
Text Completion	6
Sentence Equivalence	4
Argument Analysis	2
Reading Comprehension	8

These question types are mixed throughout their respective sections, so you may encounter them in any order. Sometimes the software groups similar questions at the beginning or the end. For example, if you're halfway through a Verbal section and haven't seen a Text Completion question, you soon will.

Scoring Max: 340 and 6

With the GRE, you receive three separate scores: Verbal, Math, and Analytical Writing. Although you get your unofficial Verbal and Math scores immediately after taking the test (as explained in the following section), you must wait 10 to 15 days to get your Analytical Writing score in the mail. The following sections explain in depth some important scoring details you may want to know.

Understanding how the scoring breaks down

On the GRE, you can score a maximum of 340 points on the multiple-choice and 6 points on the essays. Here's the scoring range for each of the three sections:

- **Verbal:** The Verbal score ranges from 130 to 170 in 1-point increments. You get 130 points if you answer just one question, which accounts for about 80 percent of a job well done. It doesn't help much, though: You need to score as well as or better than most of the other people who took the test to improve your chances of being admitted to the school of your choice.

- **Math:** The Math score also ranges from 130 to 170 in 1-point increments.

- **Analytical Writing:** You get 1 to 6 points per essay, with 6 being the highest. Each essay is graded separately, first by a trained evaluator and then by a computerized essay-grading system. Your score for that essay is the average of the two. If the two scores are very different, then another human grader steps in, and your score for that essay is the average of the two human scores. Finally, the scores of your two essays are averaged for your Analytical Writing score of 1 to 6. Essay responses that are blank or off-topic receive a score of 0. (The paper version of the GRE essay is scored only by people, not the computerized system.)

So in essence, if you perfectly ace the Verbal and Math sections, you get 170 points for each, for a total of 340. If you're perfect on the two essays, you can get an essay score of 6. The three scores are separate: You get a Math score and a Verbal score, each from 130 to 170 in 1-point increments, and an Analytical Writing score of 0 to 6, in half-point increments.

On the multiple-choice questions, you earn points only for completely correct answers. If the question requires two or more answers, you have to get all the answers correct; you don't get partial credit for a partially correct answer. However, you don't lose any points for wrong answers, so guessing behooves you. See "Playing the guessing game," later in this chapter, for more on this.

Calculating your score

Within each section, each question counts exactly the same toward your score. An easy question is worth exactly the same as a hard question. Because you can move back and forth within each section, a good strategy is to skip around and answer all the easy questions first; then go back and work the hard questions. Quite simply, in each section, the more questions you get right, the higher your score for that section.

When you complete a practice test from Part II, you can easily estimate your Math and Verbal scores. For the Math score, count the math questions you answered correctly and then add 130 to that number. Because the GRE has 40 math questions (two sections with 20 questions each), this method gives you an approximate score from 130 to 170. You can find your Verbal score the exact same way, because the GRE also has 40 Verbal questions.

The way that the computer version of the GRE calculates your scores is slightly more complicated. It takes into account the difficulty levels of the second Math and Verbal sections, weighing the scores accordingly. For example, if you do very well on the first Math section, the second Math section will be more difficult. In this second section, you may not answer as many questions correctly, but you'll have a higher score, because the GRE accounts for the increased difficulty level. However, within any section, each question counts exactly the same toward your score. The exams in this book, however, have no such adaptive mechanism, so for these, you can approximate your score by counting the correct answers.

Figuring out how your scores measure up

If you score a perfect 340 or something close to it, you know you did well. If you score a 260, you know you bombed. But what if you score something in between? Did you pass? Did you fail? What do you make of your score? Well, you can't really tell much about your score out of context. There's no pass or fail, no A, B, C, D, F — but there is a percentile ranking. To download the complete percentile table, visit www.ets.org, click GRE Tests, and search for "percentile ranking." Here are some highlights:

- ✔ A raw score of 165 is typically a 95th percentile ranking in the Verbal and a 91st percentile ranking in the Math.
- ✔ A raw score of 160 is typically an 84th percentile ranking in the Verbal and a 78th percentile ranking in the Math.

Basically, with a range of 40 points, each point counts for a lot. How well you do is relative to how well the other people taking the test perform and the requirements of the graduate program you're applying to. What's most important is that you score high enough to get accepted into the program you have your heart set on. Once you're in your program, the GRE score doesn't matter.

Your GRE score is only one part of the total application package. If you have a good undergraduate GPA, a strong résumé, and relevant work experience, you may not need as high of a GRE score. On the other hand, a stellar GRE score can compensate for your weak areas.

Playing the guessing game

The GRE doesn't penalize you by deducting points for incorrect answers, so

- ✔ If you don't know the answer, rule out as many obviously incorrect choices as possible and then guess from the remaining choices.
- ✔ Finish the section, even if you must take wild guesses near the end. Wrong answers count the same as not answering a question, so guessing on questions that you would otherwise have left blank can only help your score, not hurt it.

Seeing or canceling your scores

Immediately after finishing the GRE, you have the option of either seeing or canceling your Verbal and Math scores. Unfortunately, you don't get to see your scores first. If you *think* you had a bad day, you can cancel your test, and your scores are neither reported to the schools nor shown to you. However, the schools are notified that you canceled your test. If you choose to see your score, you see it — minus the essay scores — right away.

How much do the schools care about canceled scores? Probably not much, especially if a top GRE score (from when you retake the test 21 days later) follows the notice of cancelation. If you really want to know the impact of a canceled score, check with the admissions office of your target schools. Each school weighs canceled scores differently. See Chapter 2 for more about what to do after canceling your GRE score.

Taking advantage of the ScoreSelect option

At the end of the test, you have the option of choosing which test scores to send to your target schools, assuming that you've taken the GRE more than once (within five years). You can send the most recent scores, scores from the past, or all your test scores. However, you can't pick and choose sections from different testing dates. For example, if today's Verbal score rocked but last fall's Math score was outstanding, you can't select only those sections — you have to select the scores from one entire test. Choose to send the scores from today's test, last fall's test, or all your tests.

Gimme a Break! GRE Intermissions

The GRE provides an optional ten-minute break after the third section of the exam. However, don't expect to have the entire time to yourself: Part of that time is for checking in and out while the proctors go through their security procedures to ensure you're not bringing in any materials to cheat with. The ten-minute intermission is timed by the computer, which resumes the test whether you're seated or not. You probably have five minutes to do your business, which leaves little time to grab a bite if you're hungry. Plan accordingly with snacks and water in your locker so that during your actual five minutes, you can refresh yourself without having to scramble.

Make sure your packed snacks are light and nutritious. Sugar makes you high for a few minutes and then brings you way down. Something heavy, like beef jerky, makes you drowsy. You don't want to crash right in the middle of a quadratic equation. Take a handful of peanuts, some trail mix, or something light that isn't going to send all the blood from your brain down to your stomach for digestion.

Between other sections of the test, you get a one-minute break — just enough time to stand up and stretch a bit. You don't have time to leave your seat and come back before the test resumes. If you absolutely, positively must use the restroom and leave the computer during the test, just remember that the clock keeps ticking.

Recognizing the importance of test prep

Stories abound about how someone's friend's cousin's roommate took the GRE cold (with no preparation) and aced it. This story may be true on a very rare occasion, but you hear only the success stories. Those test-takers who took the test unprepared and bombed it don't brag about the outcome. As an instructor, however, I hear those other stories all the time.

The GRE doesn't test your intelligence; it tests how prepared you are for the test. I'd put my money on a

prepared dunce over an unprepared genius every single time. Dramatically raising a test-taker's score, say from the 30th percentile to the 90th percentile ranking, is something I do every day before breakfast, and it's what I do for you through this book. Being prepared means knowing what to expect on the test and in the questions, which means that the first time you calculate a fraction of a circle had better not be on the actual GRE. Make your mistakes *here,* in practice, *not* on the test.

Chapter 2

Owning the GRE: Strategies for Success

In This Chapter

▶ Managing your time before and during the test

▶ Deciding whether to retake the GRE

▶ Taking action if the test isn't administered properly

▶ Using scores up to five years old

The GRE isn't an IQ test. Nor is it a measure of your worth as a human being or a predictor of your ultimate success in life. The GRE is designed to assess your ability to excel in grad school by sizing you up in three areas:

✔ **Work ethic:** How hard you're willing and able to work to achieve an academic goal — in this case, performing well on the GRE — determines your work ethic. Graduate schools consider this to be a measure of how hard you'll work in their program.

✔ **Study skills:** To do well on the GRE, you must master some basic study skills and be able to process and retain new information.

✔ **Test-taking ability:** Your test-taking ability is your ability to perform well on a test, under pressure, which is a separate ability from being able to answer the questions. Exams are an essential part of grad school, so you need to prove that you can take a test without folding under pressure.

This book can't help you in the first area; that's all you. As a study guide, however, this book shapes you up in the second and third areas, enabling you to study more effectively and efficiently and improve your overall test-taking skills. By familiarizing yourself with the types of material on the exam and taking the practice tests, you establish a foundation for doing well on the GRE.

This chapter is designed to take your study skills and test-taking ability to the next level. To beat the GRE at its game, you need to maximize the use of your time, focus on key areas, and apply strategies to answer the questions quickly and correctly. This chapter shows you how to do all these things and provides you with a Plan B — what to do if things don't go so well the first time.

Making the Best Use of Your Time

As soon as you decide to take the GRE, the clock starts ticking. You have only so much time to study, so much time to practice, and suddenly so little time before the exam is tomorrow morning. The good news: I've taken many students down this road, with great results, and here I've distilled the best of the success strategies. The following sections show you how to optimize your study and practice time so you can answer the test questions more efficiently.

Budgeting your time for studying

As an undergrad, you may have mastered the fine art of cramming the night before an exam, but that doesn't work on the GRE. This test is based less on memorization and more on skills, which take time to develop. Give yourself as much time as you can to prepare for the test. Here's what I recommend in terms of total time, the amount of that time you spend working through this book, and the amount of time to set aside per day:

- **Six to 12 weeks of total preparation:** Give yourself plenty of time to review vocabulary, practice essay writing, and brush up on math concepts; take practice tests; and review areas where you need extra preparation. Six to eight weeks works well for most people, but more time is generally better. At 12 weeks, you can do extremely well, but after 12 weeks, most people get burned out or lose interest, and they forget things they learned early on.

- **One to two weeks on this book:** Reviewing the first few chapters in this book should take no more than a week, and then you can spend a week with the two practice tests — take one, score it, and review your answers. Review the concepts you missed (if you have time), and then take the second practice test. The practice tests should each take 2.5 hours (no essays) or 3.5 hours (with essays), plus another hour or two to review the answer explanations.

  Even if you don't have a lot of time to study, taking a few practices tests can benefit you come test day. You'll at least be familiar with the format of the test and time allotment for the different subtests. Knowing what to expect when you sit down to take the GRE may ease a bit of your stress.

- **One to three hours per day, five or six days per week:** Pace yourself. I've seen too many students burn themselves out from trying to master the whole test in three days. (I hope you've given yourself a bit more time than that!) Your brain needs time to process all this new information and be ready to absorb more.

If you have only a couple of weeks to study, try to determine your weakest subject areas and spend as much time as you can studying other resources to improve your understanding and skills. If you're not sure about your weakest subject areas, take one of the practice tests in the book. After you've done some review work, take the other practice test. (Fingers crossed that you bump up your score a bit.)

Prioritize your study time and schedule daily review sessions. Otherwise, other activities and responsibilities are likely to clutter your day and push study time off your to-do list.

Budgeting your time for practice

Just because you know a subject inside and out doesn't mean you can ace a test on it. Test-taking requires a completely separate skill set. Start taking practice tests at least two weeks prior to your scheduled GRE so you have time to hone your skills, learn from your mistakes, and strengthen your weak areas.

Your proficiency with the test itself is as important as your math and verbal skills for attaining a top GRE score. As you take the practice tests, don't focus exclusively on errors you made in answering specific questions. Spend time evaluating your testing performance. What kinds of mistakes do you make two hours into the exam? Do you still try as hard at the end as you do in the beginning? Do you misread the questions or make simple math mistakes? Do you fall for traps?

In addition to working the practice tests in this book, I recommend working the free computer-based practice tests that Educational Testing Service (ETS) provides at www. ets.org. See Chapter 3 for details.

Beating the clock: Time management tips

Taking the GRE is a little like playing *Beat the Clock.* The computer provides you with a stopwatch — an on-screen clock — to time each section. Your goal is to answer as many questions correctly as quickly as possible before the clock ticks down to 0:00. You have the option of removing the clock from the screen, but I don't recommend this. Instead, make the on-screen timer familiar and comfortable (or rather, less *un*comfortable) by using a stopwatch while doing homework and practice tests. Practicing with a stopwatch is part of preparing for the test-taking experience.

The clock changes from hours:minutes to minutes:seconds during the last five minutes; this, of course, means hustle time.

Don't obsess over giving each question a specific number of seconds, but do know when to give up and come back to a question later. As long as you haven't exited a section, you can return to questions in that section. Simply click Review, click the question you want to return to, and then click Go to Question. You can also mark a question for review so it's flagged on the Review Screen. Just keep in mind that while you're on the Review Screen, the clock still ticks. (See Chapter 3 for more about the computer version of the test.)

Within each section, no question carries greater weight than any other question; easier ones are worth just as much as harder ones. A good strategy is to note on your scratch paper a question that you can't answer quickly so you can answer as many of the easy questions as possible and go back to the harder ones at the end.

Answer *every* question, even if you have to make a wild guess. You're not penalized for incorrect answers, so you may as well try. See Chapter 1 for info on how the exam is scored.

Repeating the Test

Upon completing the exam, you have the option of accepting and seeing your scores immediately or canceling the results if you're convinced you did poorly. If you cancel the results, you have two choices: Retake the test or choose another career path. Most people choose to retake.

Most test-takers who repeat the exam tend to do *much* better the second time. It's as if there's no better way to prepare for the GRE than taking the GRE. Of course, you want to avoid having to take the test a second time, but if the first round doesn't go so well, don't lose hope. Also, be sure to schedule your GRE a month before your school needs the scores. That way, if you do have to retake it, you'll still meet the application deadline. Also, just knowing you have a second chance helps ease your nerves in the first round.

If you think you underperformed on the GRE, consider the following when deciding whether to retake it and when preparing to retake the exam:

✔ **Am I repeating the test to get a certain minimum qualifying score?** If you have your heart set on a particular graduate school that requires a minimum GRE score, you may not need to take the test again and again until you get that score. Talk to the admissions folks at the school you want to attend. They weigh the GRE score along with your

GPA, résumé, and personal interests and have some flexibility when making their decision; if your score is close to the target, they may just let you in. I see it happen all the time.

✔ **Am I willing to study twice as hard, or am I already burned out?** If you put your heart and soul into studying for the exam the first time, you may be too burned out to take on another round of study and practice. After all, scores don't magically go up by themselves; improvement requires effort.

✔ **What types of mistakes did I make on the first test?** If you made mistakes because of a lack of familiarity with either the test format (you didn't understand what to do when faced with a Quantitative Comparison question) or substance (you didn't know the vocabulary words or were baffled by the geometry problems), you're a good candidate for repeating the test. If you know what you did wrong, you can mend your ways and improve your score. This is one purpose of taking and reviewing the practice tests.

After taking the actual GRE, you don't get to review the correct and incorrect answer choices. However, you can get a good sense of the types of mistakes that you're likely to make by going through the practice tests in this book and reviewing the answer explanations afterward.

✔ **Was there something beyond my control?** Maybe your nerves were acting up on the first exam, you were feeling ill, or you didn't get enough sleep the night before. In that case, by all means repeat the exam. You're bound to feel better the next time. If the test was administered poorly or in a room full of distractions, you really should consider a retake. (See the section "Reporting Test Administration Abnormalities" for details.)

✔ **Did I choke?** This happens all the time, especially on the essays at the beginning. Or you could panic on a thorny math question, spending several minutes and frazzling yourself for the rest of the test. Fortunately, choking doesn't usually happen again. Almost every test-taker I've seen choke does phenomenally better on the next try.

✔ **Did I run out of steam?** Stamina is a key factor of success on the four-hour GRE. If you don't practice writing the essays when taking the practice tests, you won't be prepared for the extra hour of work before the Math and Verbal sections. Also, because you're amped on test day, you're likely to crash faster than usual. Knowing what to expect and preparing for it could boost your score on a retest.

✔ **Am I eligible to retake the GRE?** You can take the GRE only once per 21-day period and no more than five times per rolling 12 months. If you try to take the test more often than that, you won't be stopped from registering for or taking the test, but your scores won't be reported.

Can repeating the exam hurt you? Typically, no. Most schools consider only your highest score. Find out from the individual schools you're interested in whether that's their policy; it isn't the same for every school. If you're on the borderline, or if several students are vying for one spot, sometimes having taken the exam repeatedly can hurt you (especially if your most recent score took a nosedive). On the other hand, an admissions counselor who sees several exams with ascending scores may be impressed that you stuck to it and kept trying, even if your score rose only slightly. In general, if you're willing to invest the study time and effort and take the repeat exam seriously, go for it.

All your test scores for the past five years are part of your record, but you can choose which scores to send using the ScoreSelect option, as I explain in Chapter 1. For example, if you did great in October but not so well in April, you can tell ETS to ignore the April debacle and send just the October scores. (If you cancel a score and later have second thoughts about that cancellation, you can reinstate the cancelled score up to 60 days after the test date. The service costs $30. Reinstatement takes up to two weeks.)

Reporting Test Administration Abnormalities

Your test isn't actually administered by ETS. It's administered by a company licensed by ETS, and the company is required to adhere to certain standards. If something irregular occurred during the test that you believe negatively affected your score, call the ETS complaint line at 866-756-7346. You have seven days to register a complaint, so don't delay.

One of my students was seated and ready to begin the GRE only to have the test start time delayed an hour! On top of that, a lot of noise was coming from the next room — definitely an unwarranted distraction. If something like this happens to you, you can petition to have your score withheld and for the opportunity to take the GRE again at no charge.

Using Old Scores

What if you took the GRE a long time ago when you thought you were going to grad school and then opted to take a job or start a family instead? Well, if it was within the past five years, you're in luck (assuming you scored well). The GRE folks make the scores reportable for up to five years. That means that if you're pleased with your old score, you can send it right along to the school of your choice and say adios to this book right here and now. However, if you took the test more than five years ago, you have to take it again.

You can retake the test and perhaps improve your score, but until that score's fifth birthday, it remains part of your GRE record.

Chapter 3

Gearing Up for Exam Day

In This Chapter

▶ Having everything you need for exam day

▶ Brushing up on the testing center's rules and regulations

▶ Staying in tiptop test-taking shape

▶ Rehearsing with a computerized sample test

On the day of the exam, there's no such thing as a pleasant surprise. Any surprise that you experience is just going to throw you off your game, stress you out, deplete your energy, and draw your focus away from what really matters — performing your best on the GRE. Surprises can also make you so late that you actually miss your scheduled test time.

The goal of this chapter is to help you avoid nasty surprises so you know exactly what to expect on the day of the test. This way, you can focus on the GRE in a more relaxed and confident frame of mind. Confidence comes from being prepared; if you're prepared, you're more confident.

Gathering Your Stuff the Night Before

Give yourself one less distraction the morning of the exam by figuring out where the testing center and parking facilities are and getting your stuff together the night before. The test is stressful in itself, and the last thing you need is to forget something important or spend the morning in a frantic search for the testing center or a parking space.

Here's what you need:

✔ **Authorization voucher from Educational Testing Service (ETS):** If you pay with a method other than a credit/debit card or have a disability or require certain testing accommodations, ETS provides an *authorization voucher*. Not everyone gets this voucher, but if you do, be sure to bring it with you on the day of the test.

✔ **Comfortable clothes:** Dress in layers. Testing centers can be warm or, more typically, cold. Sitting there for hours shivering won't help your performance. Dress in layers so you can be comfortable regardless of how they run the A/C.

✔ **Map or directions:** Know in advance where you're going. Drive to the testing center a few days prior to your scheduled test day to check out how long the drive is, where to park, how much parking costs, and so on. If you're taking public transportation, find out where and when you need to board the bus or train, how long the ride is, how much it costs, and where you get off.

One student had to take the test at a center in the middle of a downtown area. She had checked out the area on a Saturday, when the streets were empty and parking was ample.

On the day of the test, Monday morning, the streets were jammed and all the parking was taken. Naturally, she became stressed out before her exam, and this affected her performance. She could have avoided this situation if she'd planned extra drive time for the rush-hour traffic and found alternate places to park.

✔ **Photo ID:** You must have identification with three key elements:

- A recognizable photo

- The name you registered for the test under

- Your signature

Usually, a driver's license, passport, employee ID, or military ID does the trick. A student ID alone isn't enough (although it works as a second form of ID in case something's unclear on your first form of ID). Note that a Social Security card or a credit card isn't acceptable identification.

✔ **Water and a snack:** Bring a bottle of water and a light snack, such as an energy bar or a granola bar. Avoid snacks high in sugar, simple carbohydrates, or fats.

If you're wondering whether you need to bring scratch paper, pencils, a calculator, or anything like that, proceed to the next section.

Knowing What Not to Bring

Just as important as knowing what to bring to the testing center is knowing what not to bring. Leave these items at home, in your car, or at the door:

✔ **Books and notes:** Forget about last-minute studying. You aren't allowed to take books or notes into the testing center. Besides, if you don't know the material by that time, cramming won't help and may hurt. (One of my students almost had his test score nullified because during his break, he picked up his test-prep book that was in his testing center locker. Fortunately, he didn't *open* the book, so he was allowed to keep his test score.)

✔ **Calculator:** You aren't allowed to use your own calculator, but an on-screen calculator is available during the Math sections of the exam. One nice thing about the on-screen calculator is that it features a button that transfers the number from the calculator field to the answer space. Your handheld calculator won't do that.

✔ **Friends for support:** Leave your friends at home. ETS frowns on visitors. However, having a friend drop you off and pick you up isn't a bad idea, especially if parking is likely to be a problem, such as at a downtown testing center.

✔ **Phones and other electronics:** Mobile electronic devices, including smartphones, are strictly prohibited. You can bring these to the testing center, but they must stay in a locker while you're taking the GRE. And because you can't use these devices during the test, don't use them while taking practice tests.

✔ **Scratch paper:** You aren't allowed to bring in your own scratch paper; the testing center provides it for you. If you run low during the test, request more from the proctor during the one-minute breaks between sections. Although you have plenty of room to do calculations and scribbling, your scratch paper stays at the testing center when you're done.

The testing center provides lockers for test-takers to store their belongings, so if you bring a purse or backpack, you'll have a secure place to keep it.

Handling unique circumstances

If you have a special circumstance or need, the GRE powers-that-be are usually very accommodating, as long as you give them a heads-up. For example, if you have a learning disability, you may be able to get additional testing time. Following is a brief list of special circumstances and how to obtain assistance for each:

✔ **Learning disabilities:** These disabilities refer to attention deficit hyperactivity disorder (ADHD), dyslexia, and other related or similar conditions. To find out whether you qualify for accommodations or a disabilities waiver of any sort, contact ETS Disability Services, Educational Testing Service, P.O. Box 6054, Princeton, NJ 08541-6054; phone 866-387-8602 (toll free) or 609-771-7780 (Monday–Friday 8:30 a.m. to 5:00 p.m. Eastern Time), TTY 609-771-7714, fax 609-771-7165; website www.ets.org/gre, email stassd@ets.org. Qualifying for accommodations is an involved process that takes time and may require significant effort on your part to gather the required documentation. If you have a qualifying disability, act sooner rather than later to find out what's required and when you need to submit your request and documentation.

✔ **Physical disabilities:** ETS tries to accommodate everyone. Folks who need special arrangements can get Braille or large-print exams, have test-readers or recorders, work with interpreters, and so on. You can get the scoop about what ETS considers to be disabilities and how the disabilities can change the way you take the GRE in the *Supplement for Test Takers with Disabilities.* This publication contains information, registration procedures, and other useful forms for individuals with physical disabilities. To get this publication, send a request to ETS Disability Services, P.O. Box 6054, Princeton, NJ 08541-6054. Or better yet, head to www.ets.org/gre and click the Test Takers with Disabilities or Health-Related Needs link. Voilà! All the info you need to know, along with contact information if you have questions or concerns.

✔ **Financial difficulties:** Until you ace the GRE, get into a top-notch graduate school, and come out ready to make your first million, you may have a rough time paying for the exam. However, fee waivers are available. Note that the waiver applies only to the actual GRE fee, not to miscellaneous fees such as the test-disclosure service, hand-grading service, and so on. Your college counselor can help you obtain and fill out the appropriate request forms. (If you're not currently in college, a counselor or financial aid specialist at a nearby college or university may still be glad to help you. Just call for an appointment.)

Training Physically and Mentally for Test Day

Taking an intense four-hour exam is challenging both mentally and physically. Most people aren't used to concentrating at this level for such a long time. To meet the challenge, your brain needs a good supply of oxygen and nutrients, and it gets those from an active, healthy, and alert body that consumes nutritious foods and beverages. The following sections provide guidance on whipping your body into shape for test day.

Staying active

You can't just be a bookworm for the weeks before the exam. You need to stay active. Exercise helps all parts of the body and leads to clearer thinking by increasing oxygen to the brain, so get moving! You don't need to train for a marathon. Walking, swimming, jogging, yoga, Pilates, basketball, and even active video games get your body in motion and increase overall health and circulation.

Eating well

Certain foods and beverages affect your cognitive ability, so avoid highly processed foods and foods high in sugar, starch, or fat. These foods tend to make you feel sluggish or result in brief highs followed by prolonged crashes. Lean more toward veggies, especially green, leafy veggies, and foods that are high in protein. When it comes to carbohydrates, opt for complex over simple. Complex carbohydrates are typically in fresh fruits, veggies, and whole-grain products. Simple carbohydrates (to be avoided) are in candy, soda, anything made with white flour, and most junk foods, including chips. And forget those energy drinks that combine huge amounts of caffeine and sugar to get you to a state of heightened tension.

If you plan on taking an energy drink or anything unusual on the day of the test, here's the best advice I can offer: Try it out on a practice test first. If the drink gives you the jitters or upsets your stomach, you won't want to discover this on the day of the exam.

Relaxing

Relaxation comes in many different forms for people. Some folks are relaxed when they're with friends; some read books and play music; and some do yoga, meditate, or paint. The only requirement when choosing what relaxation tool to use is making sure your brain isn't running 100 miles an hour. The whole purpose of relaxation is to give your brain a rest. So find a relaxing activity you enjoy, thank your brain by telling it to take some time off, and recharge.

Relaxation isn't a luxury — it's a requirement for both a well-balanced life and success on the GRE. You're a multifaceted human, not a work-and-study automaton. Check out the free online article at www.dummies.com/extras/gre for some hands-on ways to relax before the test.

I've seen students who are so overextended and overachieving that they stress themselves out for the test. They have trouble concentrating, get panic attacks, and generally exhaust themselves. One sure sign of the mix of panic and exhaustion is the tendency to overanalyze simple questions. If you can't accept a simple, correct answer because you're sure there must be more to it, then it's time to take a break from studying.

Test-Driving the Computerized Version

You take the exam entirely on the computer. But even the most basic software has a learning curve, and you don't want to wait till test day to learn how the software works. Nor do you want to risk making a mistake that kills your score — such as getting stuck on a question because you forgot that you can go back to it.

To gain some experience with the computerized GRE, take it for a test drive, using the free Powerprep II software that ETS offers for both Macs and PCs. At the time of this writing, the software features two actual GRE computer-based practice tests for you to become accustomed to the format of the computer-based test.

To download and install the most recent version of the software, go to www.ets.org/gre, click Prepare for the Test, click POWERPREP Software, and carefully follow the on-screen directions.

If you have trouble with the installation, return to the GRE site, click the link to view frequently asked questions about the Powerprep II software, and then click the Downloading/Installation link. This takes you to a page with solutions to the most common problems. Note, too, that the software activates all the computer security precautions, but it's not likely that the file will harm your computer.

When you run the software, it displays the Introduction to the Computer-based GRE revised General Test page in your default web browser. This opening page contains several tabs for accessing an overview of the test; guidance on preparing for the test; details about the Analytical Writing, Verbal Reasoning, and Quantitative Reasoning sections of the test; and details about test scores. Scroll down to the section "Practicing for the Test," click the Start Practicing Now button, and then scroll to the bottom of the resulting page and click Continue. This launches the practice test, which gives you access to a test preview tool and a timed and untimed practice test. Choose the desired practice test option and click Start Test.

The test appears just as it will on test day, with a title page and introduction. Keep clicking Continue in the upper-right corner of the screen until you reach the General Test Information. Read the information and click Continue to proceed. Use the buttons in the upper-right corner of the screen to navigate the test. Most of the buttons are self-explanatory, but these deserve special attention:

✔ **Mark:** Mark enables you to flag the question for review. The Review screen shows marked questions with a check mark next to them so you can easily pick them out from the rest of the questions in the list.

✔ **Review:** Review displays a list of questions you can return to. Click the question you want to go back to and then click the Go To Question button. You can then review the question and change your answer if desired.

✔ **Exit Section:** This button ends the section and saves your essay or answers so you can proceed to the next section. After you click this button, you can't go back to change answers or return to unanswered questions in the section.

✔ **Quit Test:** This button ends the test prematurely, canceling your scores. You usually want to avoid this button, especially during the actual test — unless, of course, you really want to stop and cancel your scores.

Take the computerized sample test not only to get a feel for the content and format of the questions but also to become accustomed to selecting answers and using the buttons to navigate. A day or two prior to the actual test, take the computerized practice test again to reorient yourself with the buttons.

Bringing the GRE into Your Comfort Zone

Panicking about the GRE is counterproductive. You want to enter the testing center feeling confident and relaxed. That means bringing the GRE into your comfort zone by having the right mindset. The following sections put the GRE in the proper perspective and serve to remind you of just how prepared you really are.

Getting familiar with subject matter and questions

The GRE focuses on a specific range of core concepts and presents questions in a fairly predictable format. Surprises are unlikely, especially if you're prepared and know what to expect.

A little self-affirmation goes a long way. In the days leading up to the test and on test day, remind yourself that you're prepared (even some preparation is better than none!). The GRE is designed to be challenging, but your preparation brings confidence. This is an opportunity to prove yourself and put into play the time and effort you invested in gearing up for the challenge.

Understanding that the GRE is only one of many admissions requirements

Although your performance on the GRE is an important qualification for admission into the graduate school and program of your choice, it's not the only factor that admissions departments consider. Your work experience, GPA, extracurricular activities (including volunteer work), and other factors that define you are also important parts of your application. Of course, you should do your very best on the test, but remind yourself that this isn't a do-or-die situation. Worst case, retake the exam. I've had plenty of students forget one of the key points I taught them in class and make a mistake on the day of the test. Next time around, they aced the exam.

Part II
Two Full-Length Practice GREs

What to Do the Night before the Test

- ✔ **Gather everything you need.** Make sure you have the directions to the test center, your picture ID, your authorization voucher from ETS, water and a snack, and your lucky socks.

- ✔ **Get a good night's sleep.** Wait until you get your passing scores to celebrate with your friends.

- ✔ **Avoid junk food.** Salty and sugary foods are the enemy and will drain your energy. Eat fruits and vegetables for fuel that will see you through the test.

In this part . . .

✔ Discover your areas of strength and weakness by taking a full-length GRE practice test or two.

✔ Determine where you went wrong (or right) by reading through answer explanations for all practice test questions.

✔ Score your test quickly with an answer key.

Chapter 4

Practice Exam 1

• •

Are you ready to take a practice GRE? Like the actual, computer-based GRE, the following exam consists of two 30-minute essays, two 30-minute Verbal Reasoning sections (20 questions each), and two 35-minute Quantitative Reasoning sections (20 questions each). The actual GRE may also include an extra Verbal or Quantitative Reasoning section, which doesn't count toward your score, but this practice exam has nothing like that.

Take this practice test under normal exam conditions and approach it as you would the real GRE:

- ✔ **Work when you won't be interrupted.** If you have to, lock yourself in your room or go to the library so your housemates won't disturb you. And turn off your cellphone.

- ✔ **Use scratch paper that's free of any prepared notes.** On the actual GRE, you receive blank scratch paper before your test begins.

- ✔ **Answer as many questions as time allows.** Consider answering all the easier questions within each section first and then going back to answer the remaining, harder questions. Because you're not penalized for guessing, go ahead and guess on the remaining questions before time expires.

- ✔ **Set a timer for each section.** If you have time left at the end, you may go back and review answers (within the section), continue and finish your test early, or pause and catch your mental breath before moving on to the next section.

- ✔ **Don't leave your desk while the clock is running on any section.** Though technically you're allowed to do this, it's not conducive to an effective time-management strategy.

- ✔ **Take breaks between sections.** Take a one-minute break after each section and the optional ten-minute break after the first Verbal section.

- ✔ **Type the essays.** Because you type the essays on the actual GRE, typing them now is good practice. Don't use software, such as Microsoft Word, with automatic spell-checker or other formatting features. Instead, use a simple text editor, such as Notepad, with copy and paste but no other features. The GRE essay-writing field features undo, redo, copy, and paste functionality but nothing else.

After completing this entire practice test, go to Chapter 5 to check your answers. Be sure to review the explanations for *all* the questions, not just the ones you miss. The answer explanations provide insight and a review of various concepts. This way, too, you review the explanations for questions that you guessed correctly on.

Chances are good that you'll be taking the computerized GRE, which doesn't have answer choices marked with A, B, C, D, E, and F. Instead, you'll see clickable ovals and check boxes, fill-in-the-blank text boxes, and click-a-sentence options (in some Reading Comprehension questions). I formatted the questions and answer choices to make them appear as similar as possible to what you'll see on the computer-based test, but I had to retain the A, B, C, D, E, F choices for marking your answers.

Answer Sheet for Practice Exam 1

Section 1:
Verbal Reasoning

1. Ⓐ Ⓑ Ⓒ Ⓓ Ⓔ
2. Ⓐ Ⓑ Ⓒ Ⓓ Ⓔ
3. Ⓐ Ⓑ Ⓒ Ⓓ Ⓔ Ⓕ
4. Ⓐ Ⓑ Ⓒ Ⓓ Ⓔ Ⓕ
5. Ⓐ Ⓑ Ⓒ Ⓓ Ⓔ Ⓕ
6. Ⓐ Ⓑ Ⓒ Ⓓ Ⓔ Ⓕ Ⓖ Ⓗ Ⓘ
7. Ⓐ Ⓑ Ⓒ Ⓓ Ⓔ Ⓕ Ⓖ Ⓗ Ⓘ
8. Ⓐ Ⓑ Ⓒ Ⓓ Ⓔ
9. Ⓐ Ⓑ Ⓒ Ⓓ Ⓔ
10. Ⓐ Ⓑ Ⓒ Ⓓ Ⓔ
11. Ⓐ Ⓑ Ⓒ Ⓓ Ⓔ
12. Ⓐ Ⓑ Ⓒ Ⓓ Ⓔ
13. Ⓐ Ⓑ Ⓒ Ⓓ Ⓔ
14. Ⓐ Ⓑ Ⓒ Ⓓ Ⓔ
15. A B C
16. A B C D E F
17. A B C D E F
18. A B C D E F
19. A B C D E F
20. A B C D E F

Section 2:
Quantitative Reasoning

1. Ⓐ Ⓑ Ⓒ Ⓓ
2. Ⓐ Ⓑ Ⓒ Ⓓ
3. Ⓐ Ⓑ Ⓒ Ⓓ
4. Ⓐ Ⓑ Ⓒ Ⓓ
5. Ⓐ Ⓑ Ⓒ Ⓓ
6. Ⓐ Ⓑ Ⓒ Ⓓ
7. Ⓐ Ⓑ Ⓒ Ⓓ
8. Ⓐ Ⓑ Ⓒ Ⓓ
9. Ⓐ Ⓑ Ⓒ Ⓓ Ⓔ
10. Ⓐ Ⓑ Ⓒ Ⓓ Ⓔ
11. Ⓐ Ⓑ Ⓒ Ⓓ Ⓔ
12. Ⓐ Ⓑ Ⓒ Ⓓ Ⓔ
13. Ⓐ Ⓑ Ⓒ Ⓓ Ⓔ
14. A B C
15.
16.
17.
18. A B C
19. A B C D E F
20. A B C D E F

Section 3:
Verbal Reasoning

1. Ⓐ Ⓑ Ⓒ Ⓓ Ⓔ
2. Ⓐ Ⓑ Ⓒ Ⓓ Ⓔ
3. Ⓐ Ⓑ Ⓒ Ⓓ Ⓔ
4. Ⓐ Ⓑ Ⓒ Ⓓ Ⓔ Ⓕ
5. Ⓐ Ⓑ Ⓒ Ⓓ Ⓔ Ⓕ
6. Ⓐ Ⓑ Ⓒ Ⓓ Ⓔ Ⓕ Ⓖ Ⓗ Ⓘ
7. Ⓐ Ⓑ Ⓒ Ⓓ Ⓔ Ⓕ Ⓖ Ⓗ Ⓘ
8. Ⓐ Ⓑ Ⓒ Ⓓ Ⓔ
9. A B C
10. Ⓐ Ⓑ Ⓒ Ⓓ Ⓔ
11. Ⓐ Ⓑ Ⓒ Ⓓ Ⓔ
12. Ⓐ Ⓑ Ⓒ Ⓓ Ⓔ
13. Ⓐ Ⓑ Ⓒ Ⓓ Ⓔ
14. Ⓐ Ⓑ Ⓒ Ⓓ Ⓔ
15. A B C D E F
16. A B C D E F
17. A B C D E F
18. A B C D E F
19. A B C D E F
20. Ⓐ Ⓑ Ⓒ Ⓓ Ⓔ

Section 4:
Quantitative Reasoning

1. Ⓐ Ⓑ Ⓒ Ⓓ
2. Ⓐ Ⓑ Ⓒ Ⓓ
3. Ⓐ Ⓑ Ⓒ Ⓓ
4. Ⓐ Ⓑ Ⓒ Ⓓ
5. Ⓐ Ⓑ Ⓒ Ⓓ
6. Ⓐ Ⓑ Ⓒ Ⓓ
7. Ⓐ Ⓑ Ⓒ Ⓓ
8. Ⓐ Ⓑ Ⓒ Ⓓ
9. Ⓐ Ⓑ Ⓒ Ⓓ Ⓔ
10. Ⓐ Ⓑ Ⓒ Ⓓ Ⓔ
11. Ⓐ Ⓑ Ⓒ Ⓓ Ⓔ
12. Ⓐ Ⓑ Ⓒ Ⓓ Ⓔ
13. Ⓐ Ⓑ Ⓒ Ⓓ Ⓔ
14. A B C
15.
16.
17.
18. A B C D E F
19. A B C D E F
20. A B C

Analytical Writing 1: Analyze an Issue

Time: 30 minutes

"Television and videos are going to leave a more lasting and valid perception of our society to future generations than is literature."

Directions: Discuss the extent to which you agree or disagree with the previous statement and explain your reasoning for the position you take. In developing and supporting your position, you should consider ways in which the statement may or may not hold true and explain how those considerations shape your position.

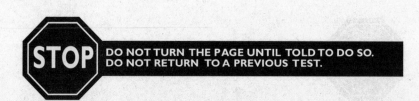

STOP DO NOT TURN THE PAGE UNTIL TOLD TO DO SO.
DO NOT RETURN TO A PREVIOUS TEST.

Analytical Writing 2: Analyze an Argument

Time: 30 minutes

The following appeared in a letter to the editor of the *Flint Herald* newspaper.

"School board elections are coming up in a few months. Voters should vote for Martinez Westwood for school board member rather than for the incumbent, Harris Blankford, because the current school board is doing a poor job. In the two years since the current board was elected, the dropout rate has increased by 30 percent, voters did not approve the necessary tax increase to raise teacher salaries, and the morale of both educators and students is down. By electing Martinez Westwood, these problems will be resolved quickly and correctly."

Directions: Write a response in which you examine the unstated assumptions of the previous argument. Be sure to explain how the argument depends on the assumptions and what the implications are if the assumptions prove unwarranted.

Section 1

Verbal Reasoning

Time: 30 minutes for 20 questions

Directions: Choose the best answer to each question. Blacken the corresponding oval(s) on the answer sheet.

Directions: For Questions 1–7, choose the one entry best suited for each blank from its corresponding column of choices.

1. The pistonless rotary engine is an automotive _____, only appearing in a select few car and motorcycle models.

Ⓐ innovation
Ⓑ anomaly
Ⓒ talisman
Ⓓ vanguard
Ⓔ paragon

2. Although the production facility emitted the foul odor, it was the residents of the community who had to _____ it, because they were powerless to do anything about it.

Ⓐ wallow in
Ⓑ circumscribe
Ⓒ stanch
Ⓓ welter in
Ⓔ bask in

3. Although he lacked the (i) _____ that he would like to have in the field, Dr. Dickstein felt confident enough of his premise to continue arguing (ii) _____ against the physician, whom he considered to be a dangerous quack and a charlatan.

Blank (i)	Blank (ii)
Ⓐ expertise	Ⓓ lackadaisically
Ⓑ fidelity	Ⓔ vehemently
Ⓒ grace	Ⓕ tentatively

4. The feeling that one is being watched is not always mere paranoia; indeed, the (i) _____ and random monitoring of citizens by some governmental bureaus is quite probably more (ii) _____ than is commonly known.

Blank (i)	Blank (ii)
Ⓐ haphazard	Ⓓ widespread
Ⓑ overt	Ⓔ surreptitious
Ⓒ intermittent	Ⓕ banal

5. At the (i) _____ of his career, Ken basks in the kudos and (ii) _____ of judges and audiences alike.

Blank (i)	Blank (ii)
Ⓐ apogee	Ⓓ reproofs
Ⓑ genesis	Ⓔ plaudits
Ⓒ nascency	Ⓕ perjury

6. Ronald Reagan considered the Iran-Contra affair to be a relatively minor (i) _____ used by his political opponents and the press to (ii) _____ him and weaken the Republican Party. Yet many experts in constitutional law viewed this and activities like it as threats to democracy itself through secrets and (iii) _____.

Blank (i)	Blank (ii)	Blank (iii)
Ⓐ breech	Ⓓ discredit	Ⓖ strategies
Ⓑ abomination	Ⓔ venerate	Ⓗ chicanery
Ⓒ transgression	Ⓕ slander	Ⓘ policies

Go on to next page ⇨

7. Myshkin, the protagonist in Dostoevsky's *The Idiot* is not so much stupid as he is (i) _____. At one point, he becomes enamored of a girl named Aglaia who (ii) _____ him for his innocence. Dostoevsky sends a clear message that a (iii) _____ individual in a corrupt world is destined to become a victim.

Blank (i)	Blank (ii)	Blank (iii)
Ⓐ dissolute	Ⓓ flouts	Ⓖ guileless
Ⓑ moronic	Ⓔ disparages	Ⓗ transparent
Ⓒ ingenuous	Ⓕ contravenes	Ⓘ feckless

Directions: Each of the following passages is followed by questions pertaining to the passage. Read the passage and answer the questions based on information stated or implied in that passage. For each question, select one answer choice unless instructed otherwise.

Community property is a legal concept that is growing in popularity in the United States. A few years ago, only the western states had community property laws, and few people east of the Mississippi had ever heard the expression "community property." Now several states have adopted or modified laws regarding community property.

Both wife and husband jointly own community property. Generally, the property that a spouse owned before the marriage is known as separate or specific property. It remains the property of the original possessor in case of a separation or divorce. Community property is anything gained by the joint effort of the spouses.

Gifts specifically bestowed upon only one party, or legacies to only one spouse, are separate property. However, courts often determine that a donor had the intention to give the gift to both parties, even though his words or papers may have indicated otherwise. Community property goes to the surviving partner in case of the death of one spouse. Only that half of the property owned by the testator can be willed away.

8. In which of the following instances would a gift to one party become community property?

Ⓐ When the court determines the intent of the donor was to make a gift to the couple

Ⓑ When the property is real (land) rather than personal (possessions)

Ⓒ When the court determines that the intent to give the gift was formed by the donor prior to the party's marriage

Ⓓ When the court determines that the gift was bestowed upon only one party

Ⓔ When the couple can use the property only when they are together

9. You may infer that the author would most likely agree with which of the following?

Ⓐ Community property is the fairest settlement concept for marital property.

Ⓑ Community property laws currently discriminate against the working spouse in favor of the homemaker spouse.

Ⓒ Community property laws will probably continue to increase in number throughout the United States.

Ⓓ Community property laws will be expanded to include all property acquired during the marriage, regardless of its source.

Ⓔ All inheritances received by one party during the marriage are in theory, if not in fact, community property.

A key study has shown that the organic matter content of a soil can be altered to a depth of 10 cm or more by intense campfire heat. As much as 90 percent of the original organic matter may be oxidized in the top 1.3 cm of soil. In the surface 10 cm, the loss of organic matter may reach 50 percent if the soil is dry and the temperature exceeds 250 degrees. The loss of organic matter reduces soil fertility and water-holding capacity and renders the soil more susceptible to compaction and erosion.

Sandy soils attain higher temperatures and retain heat longer than clay soils under similar fuel, moisture, and weather conditions. From this standpoint, it is desirable to locate campgrounds

Go on to next page ⟩

in an area with loam or clay-loam soil. Sandy soils are less susceptible to compaction damage, however, and are more desirable for campgrounds from this standpoint.

A water-repellent layer can be created in a soil by the heat from the campfire. This condition was noted only in sandy soils where the temperature remained below 350 degrees during the campfire burn. Campfires often produce temperatures above this level. By comparison, forest fires are a shorter-duration event, and soil temperatures produced are more likely to create water repellency-inducing conditions. The greater extent of forest fires makes them a more serious threat than campfires in terms of causing soil-water repellency.

If the soil remained moist for the duration of the campfire, the increased heat capacity of the soil and heat of water vaporization kept the soil temperature below 100 degrees. At this temperature, little loss of organic matter occurred, and no water repellency was created. For areas where the soil remains very moist, campfires probably have little effect on the soil properties.

Studies show that softwood fuels burn faster and produce less heat flow into the soil than do hardwood fuels under the same conditions. Elm and mesquite were the hottest burning and longest lasting fuels tested. In areas where some choice of fuels is available, the use of softwood fuels should be encouraged in an effort to minimize the effect of campfires on soil properties.

By restricting the fire site to the same area, the effects of campfires on the soil in a campground can be lessened, even if permanent concrete fireplaces are not installed. In this manner, any harmful effects are restricted to a minimum area. If campfires are allowed to be located at random by the user, the harmful effects tend to be spread over a larger part of the campground. The placement of a stone fire ring in the chosen location is one way to accomplish the objective.

These data support the decision to install permanent fireplaces in many areas and to restrict the use of campfires elsewhere in the park. This eliminates the harmful effects of campfires on the soil and allows the campground to be located on sandy soil with low compactibility and good drainage.

10. Which of the following sentences best summarizes the effect of moisture on the potential soil damage that campfires may cause?

Ⓐ If the soil remained moist for the duration of the campfire, the increased heat capacity of the soil and heat of water vaporization kept the soil temperature below 100 degrees.

Ⓑ At this temperature, little loss of organic matter occurred, and no water repellency was created.

Ⓒ For areas where the soil remains very moist, campfires probably have little effect on the soil properties.

Ⓓ Studies show that softwood fuels burn faster and produce less heat flow into the soil than do hardwood fuels under the same conditions.

Ⓔ Elm and mesquite were the hottest burning and longest lasting fuels tested.

11. The main idea of this passage is that

Ⓐ excessive campfires will eventually make it impossible to grow crops.

Ⓑ soil temperature affects soil fertility.

Ⓒ only certain woods allow for high-quality campfires.

Ⓓ soils must be able to absorb water to sustain organic matter.

Ⓔ steps can be taken to minimize soil damage from campfires.

12. Long-lasting campfires are more likely than short-lived ones to

Ⓐ create water repellency-inducing conditions.

Ⓑ maintain soil fertility.

Ⓒ occur with softwood fuels.

Ⓓ restrict damage to the top 1.3 cm of soil.

Ⓔ produce higher soil temperatures.

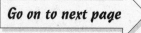*Go on to next page*

13. It can be inferred from the passage that the author would be most likely to agree with which of the following?

Ⓐ Campfires should be banned as destructive to campground soil.

Ⓑ Organic matter decreases soil erosion.

Ⓒ Clay-loam soil is preferable to sandy soil for campsites.

Ⓓ The longer the duration of the fire, the higher the resistant soil temperatures.

Ⓔ Campfires will not burn in areas with moist soil.

The best way to encourage recycling is through container deposit legislation (a bottle bill), charging a five- to ten-cent deposit on all beverage containers. Such legislation has a proven track record for increasing recycling rates for beverage containers by 75 to 95 percent, depending on the deposit amount.

14. Which of the following, if true, most effectively undermines the argument that a bottle bill is the best way to encourage recycling?

Ⓐ The money collected barely covers the cost of the additional effort.

Ⓑ Some recycling sites cannot process green plastic bottles.

Ⓒ Codes on plastic bottles make it easy for consumers to determine whether certain containers are recyclable.

Ⓓ Beverage containers account for about 5 percent of recyclable waste.

Ⓔ Charging a deposit is just another way to tax consumers.

In 1848, the Great Mahele (land division) instituted, for the first time in Hawaii, the right of individuals to own land. This was the beginning of the end for Hawaiian Sovereignty. While foreigners started buying up all the land, Hawaiians, unaccustomed to the idea of private land ownership, did not. In 1893, after the Hawaiian Monarchy was overthrown and Queen Liliuokalani was taken prisoner, the new government instituted a democracy in which only land owners had the right to vote. With no land and no voting rights, native Hawaiians had little power to restore Hawaiian Sovereignty.

For Question 15, consider each answer choice separately and select all answer choices that are correct.

15. Which of the following contributed to the end of Hawaiian Sovereignty?

Ⓐ Restricting the right to vote only to landowners

Ⓑ The overthrow of the Hawaiian Monarchy

Ⓒ Private land ownership

Directions: Each of the following sentences has a blank indicating that a word or phrase is omitted. Choose the two answer choices that best complete the sentence and result in two sentences most alike in meaning.

16. After 20 days of pouring rain, the crops were devastated — distraught farmers had no other recourse than to shout _____ at the heavens.

Ⓐ exhortations

Ⓑ imprecations

Ⓒ admonitions

Ⓓ blasphemies

Ⓔ execrations

Ⓕ excoriations

17. While the public expects professional athletes to perform incredible feats, it also expects them to do so without performance-enhancing drugs or other such substances; therefore, athletes who are caught violating the rules often suffer public _____ for doing so.

Ⓐ defamation

Ⓑ opprobrium

Ⓒ slander

Ⓓ disparagement

Ⓔ ignominy

Ⓕ libel

Go on to next page

18. Most participating businesses embrace college internship programs, and for a modest investment of time and effort, businesses obtain workers who not only are knowledgeable and skilled but also perform their tasks with _____.

    A enthusiasm ✓

    B indolence

    C competence

    D torpor

    E aptitude

    F alacrity

19. To save costs and facilitate mediation, conflicting parties often agree to hire _____ third party for resolving outstanding issues.

    A an impersonal

    B an aloof

    C a disinterested

    D an impartial

    E a biased

    F a predisposed

20. With the goal of _____ violence, the reprobates whipped the crowd into a frenzy.

    A quelling

    B fomenting

    C mollifying

    D goading

    E anticipating

    F instigating

STOP DO NOT TURN THE PAGE UNTIL TOLD TO DO SO.
DO NOT RETURN TO A PREVIOUS TEST.

Section 2

Quantitative Reasoning

Time: 35 minutes for 20 questions

Notes:

- All numbers used in this exam are real numbers.
- All figures lie in a plane.
- Angle measures are positive; points and angles are in the position shown.

Directions: For Questions 1–8, choose from the following answer choices:

- Ⓐ *Quantity A is greater.*
- Ⓑ *Quantity B is greater.*
- Ⓒ *The two quantities are equal.*
- Ⓓ *The relationship cannot be determined from the information given.*

1.

Quantity A	***Quantity B***
$\dfrac{50!}{46!}$	49^4

2.

Quantity A	***Quantity B***
$\dfrac{\sqrt{60}}{\sqrt{15}}$	2

3. The perimeter of a certain isosceles right triangle is $2+2\sqrt{2}$.

Quantity A	***Quantity B***
One side of the right triangle	$\sqrt{2}$

4. Two standard six-sided dice are thrown.

Quantity A	***Quantity B***
The probability that the dice will show doubles	$\dfrac{1}{12}$

5.

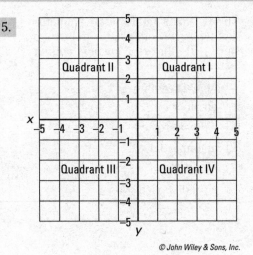

© *John Wiley & Sons, Inc.*

In this *xy*-coordinate plane, line ℓ (not shown) has a slope of 1.

Quantity A	***Quantity B***
The probability that line ℓ passes through Quadrant III	1

6. A right circular cylinder has a radius of 3 and a volume of 36π.

Quantity A	***Quantity B***
The height of the cylinder	6

7.

Quantity A	***Quantity B***
144^5	12^{10}

Go on to next page

8.

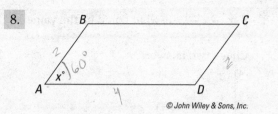

© John Wiley & Sons, Inc.

In parallelogram *ABCD*, *x* = 60, *AB* = 2, and *AD* = 4

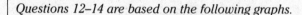

Quantity A

Quantity B

The area of parallelogram *ABCD*

$4\sqrt{3}$

9. If 225 is the average of eight consecutive even integers, which of the following is the highest of these integers?

Ⓐ 229

Ⓑ 230

Ⓒ 231

Ⓓ 232

Ⓔ 234

10. If a committee of 12 members were to choose a president, vice president, and secretary from the committee and each member can hold only one position, in how many ways can these roles be assigned?

Ⓐ 220

Ⓑ 320

Ⓒ 440

Ⓓ 1,320

Ⓔ 1,440

11. Which is closest to the standard deviation of the numbers 13, 14, 16, 18, and 19?

Ⓐ 2

Ⓑ 5

Ⓒ 8

Ⓓ 12

Ⓔ 16

Questions 12–14 are based on the following graphs.

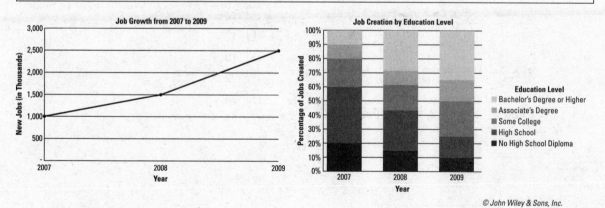

© John Wiley & Sons, Inc.

Note: Graphs drawn to scale.

12. How many more new jobs were created for graduates with a bachelor's degree or higher in 2009 than were created for the same group in 2007?

Ⓐ 77,500

Ⓑ 775,000

Ⓒ 875,000

Ⓓ 7,750,000

Ⓔ 775,000,000

13. If the total job growth number for 2009 were actually 500,000 less than the number stated in the graph, what would be the ratio of new jobs for those with only some college to new jobs for those with no college in 2009?

Ⓐ 1:1

Ⓑ 5:3

Ⓒ 5:2

Ⓓ 3:1

Ⓔ 7:2

Go on to next page ⟶

14. Which of the following statements can be inferred from the data shown in the graphs?

    Check all that apply.

    A Fewer jobs were created for those with no high school diploma in 2009 than in 2008.

    B In 2009, more than half the new jobs required a college degree.

    C Job seekers without at least some college had slightly less difficulty finding jobs in 2009 than in 2007.

15. $\dfrac{2^{10} - 2^8}{2^7 \times 3} =$

16. If an auto dealer discounts the price of a $20,000 car by 10% and then reduces the amount of the discount by 25%, what is the final asking price of the car, before taxes and fees?

17. In the given sequence a_1, a_2, a_3, a_4, where $a_1 = 1$ and $a_{n+1} = 2a_n + 2$, what is the value of a_4?

18. If $x^2 - x - 2 = 0$, what could be the value of x?

    Check two answers.

    A 2

    B 1

    C −1

19. In the given sequence $a_1, a_2, a_3, a_4, a_5, \ldots, a_n$, where $a_1 = 2$, n is a positive integer, and $a_{n+1} = 3a_n + 2$, which of the following could be a value of a_n?

    Select all that apply.

    A 2

    B 6

    C 8

    D 10

    E 26

    F 28

20. The lengths of two sides of a triangle are 5 and 7. Which of the following could be the perimeter of the triangle?

    Select all that apply.

    A 14

    B 17

    C 19

    D 22

    E 24

    F 27

STOP DO NOT TURN THE PAGE UNTIL TOLD TO DO SO. DO NOT RETURN TO A PREVIOUS TEST.

Section 3
Verbal Reasoning

Time: 30 minutes for 20 questions

Directions: Choose the best answer to each question. Blacken the corresponding oval(s) on the answer sheet.

Directions: For Questions 1–7, choose the one entry best suited for each blank from its corresponding column of choices.

1. Playing devil's advocate, the professor _____ the theory of evolution in order to challenge her students to present evidence supporting it.

Ⓐ espoused
Ⓑ subverted
Ⓒ abrogated
Ⓓ championed
Ⓔ oppugned

2. Conflict of interest is _____ in any organization that conducts its own internal investigations. Although these conflicts of interest rarely occur, the risk is ever-present.

Ⓐ rampant
Ⓑ inherent
Ⓒ extrinsic
Ⓓ prevalent
Ⓔ flagrant

3. Everyone generally agreed with the proposal, save one sticking point. To move forward with what was agreed upon, the committee decided to hold that one issue in _____ until the next meeting.

Ⓐ rectitude
Ⓑ solidarity
Ⓒ remission
Ⓓ abeyance
Ⓔ resolution

4. At many colleges and universities, student athletes must be the most (i) _____ in both their physical conditioning and studies. Coaches and professors have little patience with (ii) _____ individuals.

Blank (i)	Blank (ii)
Ⓐ assiduous	Ⓓ indolent
Ⓑ languid	Ⓔ industrious
Ⓒ studious	Ⓕ vacuous

5. A low-pass filter is one that allows low-frequency signals to pass through it while (i) _____ the amplitude of high-frequency signals. The function of such a filter may be considered (ii) _____ that of a muffler.

Blank (i)	Blank (ii)
Ⓐ mitigating	Ⓓ synonymous with
Ⓑ attenuating	Ⓔ parallel to
Ⓒ intensifying	Ⓕ analogous to

6. Initially, Bartleby the scrivener performed his job duties (i) _____ and was generally a (ii) _____ employee. That changed one day when the lawyer who hired him asked him to examine a document. Bartleby responded by saying, "I would prefer not to." Although the lawyer was somewhat taken aback by Bartleby's (iii) _____, he also found it somewhat intriguing.

Blank (i)	Blank (ii)	Blank (iii)
Ⓐ pedantically	Ⓓ meek	Ⓖ deference
Ⓑ surreptitiously	Ⓔ obdurate	Ⓗ impertinence
Ⓒ meticulously	Ⓕ tractable	Ⓘ persistence

Go on to next page ➡

7. Mr. Wilson was known in the neighborhood as an evil tyrant. He habitually (i) _____ his children and was downright (ii) _____ when speaking to his wife. Surprisingly, at least on the surface, family members seemed (iii) _____ to his erratic behaviors and abusive tirades.

Blank (i)	Blank (ii)	Blank (iii)
(A) berated	(D) slanderous	(G) trained
(B) placated	(E) vituperative	(H) subservient
(C) reproached	(F) officious	(I) inured

Directions: Each of the following passages is followed by questions pertaining to the passage. Read the passage and answer the questions based on information stated or implied in that passage. For each question, select one answer choice unless instructed otherwise.

In many ways, a Cherokee woman in the time of the "Wild West" had more power within her social group than did a European woman. It was through the mother of the family that membership in clans and general kinship were determined. A Cherokee woman was not forced to marry someone whom her family had chosen in advance for her, as was the practice in European families. Instead, the Cherokee woman had the right to choose her own mate. That mate then had the job to build a house for the woman, which was considered the woman's property. If the woman already had a house of her own, the man would go live there. Should the man be unable or unwilling to build a house, the couple would live with the woman's parents.

A Cherokee house was wattle and daub. Often described as looking like an upside-down basket, it was a simple circular frame with interwoven branches. The house was plastered with mud and sunken into the ground. Although many people do not associate log cabins with Native Americans, these dwellings became common among the Cherokee later in their history. They also built large council houses to keep the sacred fire, which was never allowed to go out.

Divorce was very simple. The woman would place her husband's possessions outside of the house, which was considered sufficient notice to free both the woman and the man to remarry. The woman kept the house her husband built for her. It was accepted for a woman to have one husband after another. Adultery in the marriage, therefore, was relatively uncommon.

Any children born to the couple were considered the woman's as well. The father had very few child-rearing responsibilities; instead, the mother and her brothers took charge of the children, showing them the tribal ways. The woman also controlled how many children would survive. She had the legal right to destroy any children who were not born healthy or give away any children she felt were beyond the number she was capable of feeding and caring for. The father had no such right.

Rights for women were just one aspect of the Cherokee civilization. During the early 1800s, the Cherokee developed a formal written constitution. Cherokees had their own courts and schools, considered by some to be of a higher standard than those of their White counterparts. Even today, the Cherokee level of education and living standard ranks among the highest of all Native American tribes.

8. The passage serves primarily to

   (A) ridicule the idea that Cherokee women were less advanced than White women.

   (B) compare and contrast the educational systems of Cherokees and Whites.

   (C) praise the advances that Cherokees made in the face of White resistance.

   (D) inform the reader of the rights of Cherokee women.

   (E) refute the theory that Cherokee women were less capable of fighting than were Cherokee men.

For Question 9, consider each answer choice separately and select all answer choices that are correct.

9. Which of the following questions is answered in the passage?

   A When did the Cherokee nation begin following a written constitution?

   B How is a Cherokee house constructed?

   C How did a Cherokee woman choose a mate?

Go on to next page

10. The author's strategy in this passage is best described as

   (A) presenting a chronological history of events.

   (B) presenting and then refuting a theory.

   (C) proposing a theory and then anticipating a counter-theory.

   (D) stating an idea and then giving supporting examples.

   (E) refuting a controversial idea.

Although citizens generally abhor any consideration of new taxes, taxes are essential in generating revenue for local, state, and federal governments. With state budgets about to go bust and more and more business being conducted online, it's imperative that e-commerce transactions be taxed in all states and at the same rate. This is the only truly fair solution.

The reasons for this are numerous. First, states can't afford the increasing loss of revenue. Second, taxing online and offline transactions equally enables brick-and-mortar businesses to compete on a level playing field. It's also more equitable for elderly consumers, who are more likely to purchase goods from local establishments. Finally, a uniform sales tax for all states prevents businesses from gaining an unfair advantage simply because they're located in a state with a low sales tax.

11. Which sentence best summarizes the author's view of the issue?

   (A) Although citizens generally abhor any consideration of new taxes, taxes are essential in generating revenue for local, state, and federal governments.

   (B) With state budgets about to go bust and more and more business being conducted online, it's imperative that e-commerce transactions be taxed in all states and at the same rate.

   (C) Second, taxing online and offline transactions equally enables brick-and-mortar businesses to compete on a level playing field.

   (D) It's also more equitable for elderly consumers, who are more likely to purchase goods from local establishments.

   (E) Finally, a uniform sales tax for all states prevents businesses from gaining an unfair advantage simply because they're located in a state with a low sales tax.

12. Which of the following, if true, most effectively challenges one of the reasons presented in the passage for charging sales tax on Internet transactions?

   (A) Most states collect property taxes.

   (B) Local businesses have higher overhead.

   (C) Collecting sales tax on the Internet is a logistical challenge.

   (D) Shipping fees typically exceed sales tax.

   (E) The Internet has a long tradition of operating tax free.

While the media blame the record number of foreclosures over the past two years on the recession, they overlook the root cause: mortgage and real estate fraud. Just before the housing bubble burst, fraud was rampant. Being greedy and pushed by the federal government to make home loans available to more people, mortgage brokers and loan offers often instructed borrowers to bend the truth on loan applications or simply sign an application with blanks, so the loan officer could fill them in with income and asset values that would "make it work."

To exacerbate the problem, buyers, sellers, real estate agents, mortgage lenders, and appraisers often conspired to engage in "innocent" cash back at closing schemes. Buyers would agree to pay more than the home's true market value, and sellers would kick back the excess amount to the buyers. This enabled the sellers to get their asking price while putting cold hard cash in the pockets of the buyers. This practice contributed significantly to artificially inflating housing prices and expanding the bubble.

Plenty of laws and regulations were already in place to discourage these types of fraud, but ever-rising housing prices hid the problem; that is, until the bubble burst.

Go on to next page

13. Which of the following, if true, adds support to the claim that rampant fraud was the root cause of the foreclosure crisis?

    Ⓐ Many buyers borrowed significantly more to purchase a home than they could make payments on.

    Ⓑ Mortgage brokers and loan officers are paid on commission, often based on the volume of loans they approve.

    Ⓒ Many appraisers wrote appraisals for the amount homeowners or buyers wanted to borrow rather than the home's market value.

    Ⓓ Many homeowners who had cashed out the equity in their homes owed more than their homes were worth when prices dropped.

    Ⓔ Many home buyers took out adjustable rate mortgages when rates were low. When rates rose, they could no longer afford the payments.

According to statistics from the Organization for Economic Co-Operation, the average workweek for U.S. workers was 35 hours and dropped to 33 hours during the recent recession. If you think that sounds low, consider Spain, Denmark, and Ireland, where the average worker puts in 31 hours a week, or the Netherlands and Norway, with an average workweek of 27 hours! Some claim even that's too long. According to Eric Rauch from MIT, "An average worker needs to work a mere 11 hours per week to produce as much as one working 40 hours in 1950." That would mean returning to a 1950s standard of living, but other countries with that same standard of living are no less satisfied than the average American.

14. Which of the following best summarizes the main idea of this passage?

    Ⓐ The workweek should be shortened to 11 hours.

    Ⓑ The time to shorten the workweek has arrived.

    Ⓒ Shortening the workweek reduces the quality of life.

    Ⓓ European countries are more progressive than the United States.

    Ⓔ The average worker is nearly four times more productive now than in 1950.

Directions: Each of the following sentences has a blank indicating that a word or phrase is omitted. Choose the two answer choices that best complete the sentence and result in two sentences most alike in meaning.

15. Venezuelan President Hugo Chavez was a passionate speaker well known for his _____ against imperialism and the United States.

    A discourses
    B harangues
    C homilies
    D platitudes
    E diatribes
    F parables

16. In 2001, Afghanistan's puritanical Taliban Islamic militia, ignoring international protests, embarked on what can only be described as _____ mission to destroy ancient religious statues, including two towering stone statues of Buddha.

    A a bombastic
    B an iconoclastic
    C a deleterious
    D a pestilential
    E a sacrilegious
    F an antagonistic

17. A politician or celebrity is often held to high standards in relation to his public comments, and even an intelligent individual can be called _____ for a minor slip of the tongue.

    A inane
    B fatuous
    C astute
    D preposterous
    E perspicacious
    F outlandish

Go on to next page

18. The series name *For Dummies* is based on the premise that anyone is a dummy in a subject area in which he is neither trained nor educated; thus, even intelligent _____ are dummies.

    A doyens

    B gurus

    C incompetents

    D fledglings

    E plebeians

    F neophytes

19. Many patients seeking treatment for depression report symptoms of _____ even though they are getting plenty of sleep.

    A lassitude

    B liquidity

    C idleness

    D listlessness

    E melancholy

    F vivaciousness

> *Read the passage and answer the question based on information stated or implied in the passage.*

> *The following passage is taken from* Skywatchers, Shamans & Kings: Astronomy and the Archaeology of Power, *by E. C. Krupp (Wiley).*

Now, to understand the power of sacred cities and cosmic shrines we have to understand the power of the cosmos. The ancients recognized that there is really only one thing taking place in the universe, one expression of transcendental power, and that is change. Day transforms into night. Each night alters the shape of the moon. Seasons change. Seeds sprout into the light and gradually grow into mature plants that flower and blow to seed. Through metamorphosis, tadpoles become frogs, and caterpillars become moths. Our lives change. Clothes, language, music, and automobiles all go out of style. New cars inevitably age and betray their mileage. The world changes. Landslides recontour the cliffs. Rivers flood and occupy new grooves. The tide leaves and returns.

20. Which of the following best summarizes the main point of the passage?

    Ⓐ The power of sacred cities and cosmic shrines is evident through the continual changes we observe around us.

    Ⓑ The world is in a continual state of flux.

    Ⓒ The power of the cosmos is evident through the continual changes we observe around us.

    Ⓓ The world is in a constant state of change, so people must learn to adapt.

    Ⓔ Change is evident in everything from changing seasons to changing styles.

STOP DO NOT TURN THE PAGE UNTIL TOLD TO DO SO. DO NOT RETURN TO A PREVIOUS TEST.

Section 4

Quantitative Reasoning

Time: 35 minutes for 20 questions

Notes:

- ✔ All numbers used in this exam are real numbers.
- ✔ All figures lie in a plane.
- ✔ Angle measures are positive; points and angles are in the position shown.

Directions: For Questions 1–8, choose from the following answer choices:

- Ⓐ *Quantity A is greater.*
- Ⓑ *Quantity B is greater.*
- Ⓒ *The two quantities are equal.*
- Ⓓ *The relationship cannot be determined from the information given.*

1.

Quantity A	**Quantity B**
$\sqrt{(97)(98)(99)(100)}$	10,000

2. For all positive integers n and p, where $n > p$, $n \therefore p = \dfrac{n}{p+n}$.

Quantity A	**Quantity B**
The lowest possible value of $n \therefore p$	0.5

3. From a group of ten members, three will be sent to represent the group at a meeting.

Quantity A	**Quantity B**
The number of different possibilities for the group with no regard to order	720

4. To create a 1.5% saline solution, a chemist mixes a number of parts of a 1.0% solution with a number of parts of a 2.0% solution.

Quantity A	**Quantity B**
The number of parts of 1.0% solution needed	The number of parts of 2.0% solution needed

5.

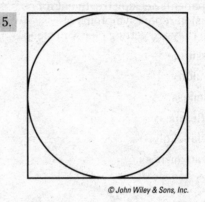

© John Wiley & Sons, Inc.

The circle is inscribed within the square of area 16.

Quantity A	**Quantity B**
The fraction of the square covered by the circle	$\dfrac{3}{4}$

6.

Quantity A	**Quantity B**
The longest distance between any two points of a cube of volume 8	$2\sqrt{3}$

7.

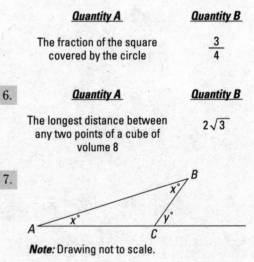

Note: Drawing not to scale.

© John Wiley & Sons, Inc.

Quantity A	**Quantity B**
$2x$	y

Go on to next page

8. Andrew is five years older than Carl, and in five years, Carl's age will be 20% less than Andrew's age.

Quantity A	*Quantity B*
Andrew's age in five years	20

9. If the volume of a cube is 27, what is the surface area?

Ⓐ 18

Ⓑ 27

Ⓒ 36

Ⓓ 45

Ⓔ 54

10. A lottery machine randomly selects three balls, one at a time and without replacement, from n balls in a barrel. The balls are labeled numerically 1 through n, with no two balls the same. If an employee adds one more uniquely numbered ball to the barrel, in terms of n, how many three-number combinations can be produced by the lottery machine?

Ⓐ $n(n^2 - 1)$

Ⓑ $n(n^2 - 2)$

Ⓒ $n(n^2 - 3n - 2)$

Ⓓ $n(n^2 - 2n - 2)$

Ⓔ $n(n^2 - 2n - 1)$

11.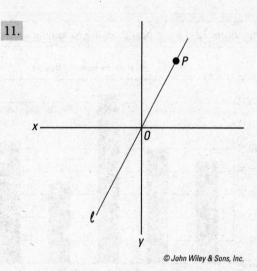

© John Wiley & Sons, Inc.

In this xy-coordinate plane, line ℓ passes through both the origin and Point P. If the (x, y) coordinates of Point P are $\left(1, \sqrt{3}\right)$, how far is Point P from the origin?

Ⓐ 1

Ⓑ $\sqrt{3}$

Ⓒ 1.5

Ⓓ 2

Ⓔ $2\sqrt{2}$

Go on to next page

Questions 12–14 are based on the following graphs.

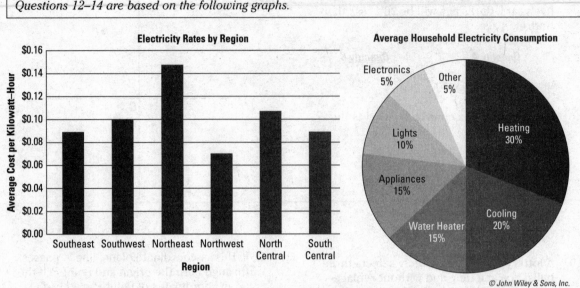

Electricity Rates by Region

Average Household Electricity Consumption

© John Wiley & Sons, Inc.

Note: Graphs drawn to scale.

12. Assuming the average household uses 15 kilowatt-hours (kWh) of electricity per day to heat its home, approximately how much would the average household pay for electricity per year if located in the northeast region?

   Ⓐ $1,500

   Ⓑ $1,800

   Ⓒ $2,200

   Ⓓ $2,700

   Ⓔ $3,200

13. The Joneses live in the north central region. After paying a whopping $4,500 on electricity last year, they installed a new geothermal furnace and extra insulation at a cost of $8,000 total, which cut their heating bill by 35%. At this rate, about how many years will it take them to recoup their investment?

   Ⓐ 16

   Ⓑ 12

   Ⓒ 8

   Ⓓ 6

   Ⓔ 3

14. Based solely on data shown in the graphs, which of the following statements are true?

   Check all that apply.

   Ⓐ Cooling a home in the northeast costs more than heating a home in the northwest.

   Ⓑ Cutting electricity usage from 75 kWh per day to 50 kWh per day would result in an annual savings of between $800 and $900 in the southwest.

   Ⓒ Moving from the northeast to the south central region while still using 50 kWh of electricity per day would result in an annual savings of more than $400 in heating alone.

15. $\dfrac{2^{11} - 2^{10}}{2^{10}} =$

16. What is the smallest prime factor of 210,423?

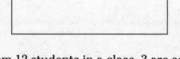

17. From 12 students in a class, 3 are selected to attend a meeting. If the order of selection does not matter, how many possible groups can be selected?

18. A set of numbers contains only 3, 4, 5, 6, and 7. If integer x is added to the set, bringing the range to 8, which of the following *could* be the new average (arithmetic mean)?

Select all that apply.

- [A] 4
- [B] 5
- [C] 6
- [D] 7
- [E] 8
- [F] 9

19. If a right circular cylinder has a height of 4 and a radius of n, where n is a positive integer, which of the following could be the volume?

Select all that apply.

- [A] 4π
- [B] 8π
- [C] 9π
- [D] 13π
- [E] 16π
- [F] 20π

20. If the positive integer x is a multiple of 8 and the positive integer y is a multiple of 12, then which of the following *must* be true?

Select two answers.

- [A] xy is a multiple of 24
- [B] $\frac{xy}{16}$ is an odd number
- [C] $\frac{3y}{9}$ is an integer

STOP DO NOT TURN THE PAGE UNTIL TOLD TO DO SO. DO NOT RETURN TO A PREVIOUS TEST.

Chapter 5

Practice Exam 1: Answers and Explanations

· ·

After taking Practice Exam 1 in Chapter 4, use this chapter to check your answers and see how you did. Carefully review the explanations because doing so can help you understand why you missed the questions you did and also give you a better understanding of the thought process that helped you select the correct answers. If you're in a hurry, flip to the end of the chapter for an abbreviated answer key.

Analytical Writing Sections

Essay writing (and scoring) is subjective to some degree. There's no right or wrong answer, and every essay is slightly different. Evaluators, however, have a checklist of specific criteria for grading your essay. To check your own essay, consider the following questions:

✔ **Did you follow the instructions?** The prompt tells you what to do. For example, an Argument Analysis prompt may ask you to consider ways in which the argument relies on certain unstated assumptions, or it may instruct you to describe circumstances in which taking a certain course of action would or would not be best. To score well, you need to follow those instructions and write about what the prompt asks for.

✔ **Have you taken a clear stand in your essay?** Although arguing both sides of an issue or discussing strengths and weaknesses is fine, you must make your opinion or position clear. Don't expect the evaluators to infer your position. Be sure to *declare* your opinion in your introduction and be *consistent* throughout your essay.

✔ **Did you back up your stance with specific examples?** Anyone can state a position, but you must support your position with specific examples. You don't have to be right, but you do need to provide solid support for your claim. Also make sure your examples aren't easily refutable.

✔ **How quickly did you get to the point in each paragraph?** The evaluator will always look for your point in the first two lines of each paragraph, so don't try to be clever and write a paragraph with a surprise ending or twist. State clearly and unequivocally in the first line of each paragraph the point of that paragraph. Then spend the rest of the paragraph supporting that point.

✔ **Have you stayed on topic?** After stating your position in the introductory paragraph, make sure each succeeding paragraph supports that position instead of wandering off topic. Each paragraph should have a sentence (preferably at the end) that ties the paragraph directly to your position statement.

✔ **Did you avoid fluff?** Though longer essays typically earn higher scores, the higher scores are due to the fact that the essay provides sufficient support, not because it rambles on and on. Your essay won't be judged on word count; it will be judged on how sufficiently you explore the topic.

✔ **Does your essay maintain a professional tone?** The essay section isn't for creative writing. It's more like business writing, so avoid off-color language, slang, and inappropriate humor.

Section 1: Verbal Reasoning

1. **B.** An *anomaly* is something that stands out as being different. The rotary engine, appearing in only a few models, is such. It may also be an *innovation* or a *paragon* (model of excellence), but those don't support the meaning of the sentence. *Talisman* (good-luck piece) and *vanguard* (trailblazer) don't fit.

2. **D.** *Welter* means to writhe, to pitch and toss, meaning the residents would be suffering in the odor. They certainly wouldn't *wallow* or *bask* in it, because those words imply enjoyment. They couldn't *circumscribe* (restrict) or *stanch* (stop) it, because the sentence states that they're powerless.

3. **A, E.** Focus on the second blank. If Dr. Dickstein felt that the man against whom he was arguing was dangerous, he'd argue *vehemently* (strongly) against him. Eliminate *lackadaisically,* which means in a mellow, laid-back, nonenergetic way, and *tentatively,* which means hesitantly or uncertainly. If he felt confident enough to argue, which implies he wasn't confident otherwise, he must have been lacking in *expertise* (skill and knowledge). Neither *fidelity* (faithfulness) nor *grace* (elegance) is a good match for the first blank.

4. **C, D.** Start with the second blank. Say, "The practice is probably more *common* than realized." *Widespread* means common, spread about everywhere. *Surreptitious* means sneaky, and *banal* means boring, neither of which is a good fit for the second blank. Choose the right word for the first blank by the process of elimination. *Haphazard* (random, chaotic) or *overt* (out in the open) monitoring of citizens doesn't describe the type of secretive activity being alluded to here, making *intermittent* (occasional) the only sensible choice.

5. **A, E.** Start with the second blank. If Ken *basks* in something, he enjoys it immensely, so it must be good. You can deduce the same thing by knowing that *kudos* means praise, glory, fame. The word that goes with "kudos and . . ." must be positive as well. *Plaudits* are praises, whereas *reproofs* are criticisms and *perjury* is lying. To earn these praises, Ken must have been at the *apogee* (highest point of his career), not the *genesis* (beginning) or *nascency* (infancy).

6. **C, D, H.** Reagan may have considered Iran-Contra to be a minor *transgression* (wrongdoing). *Breech* (rear end) is a trap because of its similarity to *breach* (violation), which would work if it were an answer choice. *Abomination* (outrageous action) is too strong of a word to be minor. For the second blank, political opponents may use a violation to *discredit* (dishonor) someone, not *venerate* (admire) or *slander* (insult) him. For the third blank, *strategies* and *policies* are too neutral; *chicanery* (trickery), however, is something that could be a threat.

7. **C, E, G.** After reading the passage, you know that Myshkin is probably a victim as a result of something that doesn't quite rank as stupid but is close. *Moronic* would be stronger than stupid, so you can rule that out, and *dissolute* means immoral, which would be more likely to make Myshkin a criminal than a victim. So Myshkin must be *ingenuous* (gullible), and Aglaia would be more likely to *disparage* (belittle) him for his innocence than *contravene* (come in conflict with). *Flout* means to treat with disdain but is used to refer to laws, conventions, or traditions, not people. For the third blank, you're looking for a word that matches up with ingenuous, which is *guileless* (honest, straightforward), not *transparent* (obvious) or *feckless* (useless).

8. **A.** The passage states that a court may deem a gift community property if the donor's intent was to give it to both parties, even if the donor didn't state so specifically. Choice (B) is wrong, because it distinguishes between real and personal property, which isn't covered in the passage. Choice (C) is also wrong but very tricky. Nothing in the passage states that the time of the intent to make the gift is important; only the intent of the donor counts. If you picked Choice (C), you read too much into the question. You can also rule out Choice (D), because if the gift was bestowed upon only one party, it would not be considered community property. And you can rule out Choice (E), because the passage makes no mention of the communal use of property having anything to do with the property's legal ownership.

9. **C.** The author mentions early in the passage that only a few community-property states used to exist, but the number has been steadily increasing. From this fact, you may infer that this increase will continue.

   Choice (A) is definitely a judgment call. Who's to say whether the community property concept is fair, not fair, the fairest, or the least fair? Passages (unless they're editorial or opinion types, which are infrequently included on the GRE) rarely give personal opinions or push one person's theories or philosophies. Choice (B) is well outside the scope of this passage, which mentions nothing about homemakers. Choice (D) goes overboard: Just because the author believes that community-property states will grow doesn't mean states will turn *all* possessions into community property.

   Closely scrutinize any answer choices with strong words, such as *all, every, never,* and *none.* Choice (E) has this problem: It includes the excessive word *all.*

10. **C.** "For areas where the soil remains very moist, campfires probably have little effect on the soil properties." This sentence explains the effect of soil moisture on the potential damage that campfires can cause to the soil.

11. **E.** This passage contains a lot of dry detail (so to speak) about how campfires damage soil and its ability to support life, and the author uses these details to recommend a certain action. Choice (E) fits perfectly with the author's concern that campfires cause soil damage, which must be minimized. Choice (A) is too extreme. Choices (B) and (D) are true statements, but they're only two of several factors that the author mentions. Choice (C) is also a detail, but that answer is wrong, primarily because the author is concerned that burning certain types of wood leads to soil damage, not with how well the woods work for the campfire per se.

   Just because a statement is true doesn't mean it's the correct answer; in a main idea question, all five choices may in fact be true, but only *one* is the main idea.

12. **E.** Common sense suggests that Choice (E) is the right answer — a notion that's confirmed by the third paragraph, which mentions that short-lived forest fires are more likely than campfires to create water repellency-inducing conditions (knocking out Choice [A]). This information implies that campfires last longer. Combine this reasoning with the explicit mention that campfires typically exceed 350 degrees, and you've got your answer. Choice (C) is directly contradicted by the fourth paragraph, and Choices (B) and (D) don't make sense. The passage often mentions that heat flow into the soil damages it. A long-lasting campfire produces more heat flow than a short-lived one.

   Although you certainly don't need to have any background knowledge to answer Reading Comprehension questions (all the necessary info is given or implied in the passage), don't hesitate to use your common sense, especially with biological and physical science passages. Common sense is a good place to start, but do be sure to check your *obvious* answer with the facts given in the passage.

13. **B.** The last sentence of the first paragraph states that the loss of organic matter reduces water-holding capacity and renders the soil more susceptible to erosion. Note that this question basically requires you to truly understand the whole passage. If you didn't read the passage carefully but instead skimmed for specific answers to specific questions, this question would've been a good one to guess on.

14. **D.** If beverage containers account for only 5 percent of recyclable waste, then container deposit legislation would fail to address recycling issues related to 95 percent of recyclable waste. The other choices fail to address the question.

15. **A, B, C.** According to the passage, all three events contributed to Hawaii's loss of sovereignty.

16. **B, E.** *Imprecations* and *execrations* both mean curses. *Exhortations* are more for conveying urgent advice. *Admonitions* or *excoriations* are more along the lines of scolding than cursing, and *blasphemies* convey a connotation of irreverence, which makes it a poor match for either of the correct choices.

17. **B, E.** *Opprobrium* and *ignominy* convey a sense of contempt. *Defamation, slander, disparagement,* and *libel* are more along the lines of insulting someone or soiling someone's reputation.

18. **A, F.** *Enthusiasm* and *alacrity* mean eagerness. *Indolence* and *torpor* convey a sense of not being very quick to action, which wouldn't make businesses very happy. *Competence* and *aptitude* both mean knowledgeable, but the sentence indicates that the workers are not only knowledgeable but something else, too.

19. **C, D.** *Disinterested* and *impartial* describe a quality necessary for a mediator: objectivity. Someone who's *impersonal* or *aloof* (unfriendly, distant) may be impartial, too, but probably wouldn't make a very good mediator. And someone who's **biased** (partial) or *predisposed* to one side or the other would make a terrible mediator.

20. **B, F.** *Fomenting* and *instigating* suggest that the **reprobates** (morally unprincipled persons) were trying to stir up trouble, which is what rabble-rousers do. If they were **quelling** (stopping) or **mollifying** (lessening) the violence, they wouldn't be very good rabble-rousers. **Goading** (provoking) is incorrect, because you may goad a person, but you don't goad an activity, and **anticipating** (expecting) isn't even in the ballpark.

Section 2: Quantitative Reasoning

1. **B.** Quantity A reduces to $50 \times 49 \times 48 \times 47$, the average of which is less than Quantity B's average of 49.

2. **C.** Simplify the fraction in Quantity A as follows:

$$\frac{\sqrt{60}}{\sqrt{15}} = \frac{\sqrt{15} \times \sqrt{4}}{\sqrt{15}} = \sqrt{4} = 2$$

3. **C.** An isosceles right triangle is a 45-45-90 triangle, with side ratios of $x + \frac{x\sqrt{2}}{2} + \frac{x\sqrt{2}}{2}$, where x is the hypotenuse. The only way the isosceles right triangle could have a perimeter of $2 + 2\sqrt{2}$ is with a hypotenuse of 2 and sides that are each $\frac{2\sqrt{2}}{2} = \sqrt{2}$.

4. **A.** Probability comes from the number of desired outcomes divided by the number of possible outcomes. The probability of 6 doubles over 36 total possible combinations is $\frac{6}{36}$, which reduces to $\frac{1}{6}$.

5. **C.** A line with a slope of 1 goes from the lower left-hand side of the graph to the upper right-hand side. It reaches Quadrant III regardless of the y-intercept.

6. **B.** The volume of a right circular cylinder is $\pi r^2 h$. Using what you know of the cylinder, solve for h, or the height, with

$$36\pi = \pi r^2 h$$
$$36\pi = \pi 9h$$

Divide both sides by 9π, and $h = 4$.

7. **C.** Remember that 144^5 can also be written as $\left(12^2\right)^5$, which equals 12^{10}.

8. **C.** To find the area of the parallelogram, multiply the base AD by the height. The base is 4, but finding the height can be a challenge. Draw a line from Point B straight down to AD, creating a 90-degree angle with AD and a 30-60-90 triangle with a hypotenuse of 2 (segment AB). Remember the side relationships of a 30-60-90 triangle: If it has a hypotenuse of 2, then the height is $\sqrt{3}$, which is also the height of the parallelogram. The base times the height produces an area of $4\sqrt{3}$.

   This problem shows why you need to memorize the common Pythagorean ratios. Though you can always find the third side of a right triangle given the other two sides, in this example, you're given only *one* side of the 30-60-90 triangle.

9. **D.** If 225 is the average, then the two middle numbers are 224 and 226. From this, you know that all eight consecutive integers are 218, 220, 222, 224, 226, 228, 230, and 232, with 232 being highest.

10. **D.** Use the permutations formula to solve this one:

    $$_nP_k = \frac{n!}{(n-k)!}$$

    If n equals the 12 members on the committee and they're choosing $k = 3$ positions, then

    $$_{12}P_3 = \frac{12!}{(12-3)!} = \frac{12!}{9!} = \frac{12 \times 11 \times 10 \times 9!}{9!} = 12 \times 11 \times 10 = 1{,}320$$

11. **A.** To approximate the standard deviation, use the mean deviation. First, find the arithmetic mean (average) of these numbers, which is 16. Next, find the positive distances of each number from the mean, which respectively are 3, 2, 0, 2, and 3. Finally, find the average of these distances, which is 2. Note that 2 isn't the exact standard deviation, but it's close (within 1), and the question asks which answer is closest to the standard deviation.

12. **B.** Subtract the total number of new jobs created for those with a bachelor's degree or higher in 2007 from the total number for the same group in 2009. To determine the 2009 number, multiply 35%, or 0.35, by 2,500,000 to get 875,000. To determine the 2007 number, multiply 10%, or 0.10, by 1,000,000 to get 100,000. Now subtract 100,000 from 875,000 to arrive at the answer, 775,000.

13. **A.** Although the question references the first graph, the data in that graph is irrelevant. The ratio stays the same regardless of the total, unless only a certain group is affected. Look at the second graph, which shows that 25 percent of new jobs in 2009 were created for people with some college. The group with no college is made up of those who completed high school plus those with no high school diploma: $15\% + 10\% = 25\%$. The ratio of 25:25 equals 1:1.

14. **C.** Choice (A) is wrong, because although the percentage of jobs declined for those with no high school diploma, the actual number of new jobs rose. In 2009, the number of new jobs (dropping the thousands to simplify the math) is $2{,}500 \times 0.10 = 250$, while in 2008, the number of new jobs is $1{,}500 \times 0.15 = 225$; that means 25,000 fewer jobs in 2008. Choice (B) is wrong, because the second graph shows that in 2009, exactly half of the jobs required a college degree. Choice (C) is correct, because in 2009, those without at least some college had 625,000 new jobs (25% of 2,500,000), which is slightly higher than the 600,000 new jobs for the same group in 2007 (60% of 1,000,000).

15. **2.** Simplify the fraction as follows:

    $$\frac{2^{10} - 2^8}{2^7 \times 3} = \frac{2^8\left(2^2 - 1\right)}{2^7 \times 3} = \frac{2^8 \times 3}{2^7 \times 3} = \frac{2^8}{2^7} = 2$$

16. **$18,500.** A 10% discount of a $20,000 price is $2,000. A 25% reduction of the $2,000 discount brings the new discount to $1,500, for an asking price of $18,500 for the car.

17. **22.** Use the formula to find a_2 by substituting a_1 for a_n and a_2 for a_{n+1}. Now the formula becomes $a_2 = 2a_1 + 2$. Because $a_1 = 1$, $a_2 = 2(1) + 2$, or 4. Do this again with a_2 and a_3 for an a_3 value of 10 and an a_4 value of 22.

18. **A, C.** Factor the equation to $(x+1)(x-2) = 0$, giving x the two possible values of –1 and 2.

19. **A, C, E.** Use the formula to find a_2 by substituting a_1 for a_n and a_2 for a_{n+1}. Now the formula becomes $a_2 = 3a_1 + 2$. Because $a_1 = 2$, $a_2 = 3(2) + 2$, or 8. Do this again with the next few values of a, up to and through 28, because that's the highest number; a_3 has a value of 26, which makes a_4 have a much greater value than anything in the list.

20. **B, C, D.** With two sides equaling 5 and 7, the third side has to be between 2 and 12, not inclusive. This places the perimeter between 14 and 24, again not inclusive. Only three of the numbers fall within that range.

Section 3: Verbal Reasoning

1. **E.** *Oppugn* means to call into question, which the professor is doing by playing the devil's advocate. *Espoused* and *championed* mean the opposite, which doesn't make sense. *Subverted* and *abrogated* imply that the professor was able to prove the theory wrong or abolish the theory simply by declaring an end to it, but if the professor is trying to get her students to present evidence supporting the theory of evolution, then these meanings don't fit.

2. **B.** *Inherent* means by nature. *Rampant* and *prevalent* don't work, because the second sentence states that these conflicts rarely arise. *Extrinsic* would imply that the conflicts arise from outside the organization, which doesn't make sense. *Flagrant* means blatant — easily observable, which fits the first sentence but doesn't convey the sense that the risk is ever-present, as stated in the second sentence.

3. **D.** *Abeyance* means temporary inactivity. *Remission* is pretty close, but it means something more along the lines of retreating or decreasing. *Rectitude* means righteousness, *solidarity* means unity, and *resolution* means solution, which wouldn't apply to a sticking point.

4. **A, D.** Student athletes would need to be *assiduous* (hardworking), because coaches and professors have little patience for *indolent* (lazy) individuals. For the first blank, *languid* (lethargic) is the opposite of what's needed, and *studious* (diligent in studies) would apply only to studies, not to physical conditioning. For the second blank, *industrious* (hardworking) is the opposite of what's needed, and *vacuous* means clueless, which fits the second part of the sentence but doesn't go with the first part.

5. **B, F.** If a low-pass filter is *analogous to* (similar to) a muffler, it would *attenuate* (reduce) the amplitude, certainly not *intensify* (increase) it. *Mitigate* is a decent second choice, but it means something more along the lines of making something less severe. For the second blank, a filter can't possibly be considered *synonymous with* a muffler. *Parallel to* means something more along the lines of corresponding to.

6. **C, F, H.** Start at the end of the question. If the lawyer who hired Bartleby was taken aback, Bartleby probably did something bad, so that eliminates *deference* (respect) and *persistence* (diligence); he must be guilty of *impertinence* (being disrespectful). Now, because you know something changed for the worse, you know the first two blanks need positive words. Filling the first blank is fairly easy: Bartleby would've started out performing his job duties *meticulously* (carefully), not *pedantically* (overly concerned

with formalities) or **surreptitiously** (secretly). Filling the second blank is more of a challenge. Because **obdurate** (stubborn) isn't positive, you can immediately rule it out. **Meek** (gentle, perhaps overly so) and **tractable** (easily managed) are fairly close in meaning, but *tractable* is the better choice.

7. **A, E, I.** The first sentence establishes Mr. Wilson as an ogre, so you know he probably didn't speak too kindly to his wife and kids. He would **berate** (put down) his children, definitely not **placate** (pacify) them. He'd probably **reproach** (scold) them, too, but *berate* means the language he used was abusive, which it would be if he were an evil tyrant. Likewise, when speaking to his wife, he would more likely be **vituperative** (verbally abusive) than **slanderous** (speaking badly of someone) or **officious** (meddlesome). For the last blank, you know that the reactions of the wife and children were surprising or unexpected, so they would seem **inured** to (accustomed to) the abuse, not *trained* or **subservient** (submissive), which is what you would expect.

8. **D.** Because the primary purpose or main idea question is so common in Reading Comprehension passages, always read them with an eye toward identifying those points. Although this passage grows more general at the end, it's primarily about the rights of Cherokee women.

9. **A, B.** The second paragraph describes how the Cherokee house was constructed, and the last paragraph mentions that the Cherokee developed a formal written constitution sometime during the 1880s. Choice (C) is incorrect because although the passage says the Cherokee woman has the right to choose her own mate, the procedure for this decision isn't covered anywhere.

10. **D.** The best way to answer this question is by the process of elimination. The passage doesn't have a *chronology* of events, Choice (A). Nor does the passage have any *refutation* (disproving) of a theory, Choice (B), or counterexample to a theory, Choice (C). Also, the passage doesn't have proof or disproof of a controversial theory, Choice (E). All the author does is state his idea and then give examples to support what he said.

11. **B.** The second sentence tells you that "it's imperative that e-commerce transactions be taxed in all states and at the same rate."

12. **D.** The fact that shipping fees typically exceed sales tax challenges the second reason given to charge sales tax for online transactions. If shipping fees exceed sales tax, then charging e-commerce merchants sales tax wouldn't level the playing field but put e-commerce merchants at a disadvantage, because online customers would be paying shipping fees *and* sales tax. Choice (A) is wrong, because property taxes aren't mentioned and aren't relevant. Choice (B) supports the notion that charging online businesses a sales tax would help level the playing field for brick-and-mortar merchants. Choice (C) isn't mentioned and isn't relevant. You can also rule out Choice (E) due to irrelevance, because it's not mentioned in the passage, and tradition has nothing to do with whether changing a tax policy is a good idea.

13. **C.** Choice (C) is an example of fraud, because appraisals should reflect the market value of the home, not how much buyers want to borrow. All the other choices present factors that possibly contributed to the foreclosure crises, but they fail to describe any activity that could be considered illegal.

14. **B.** The passage suggests that the workweek be shortened without specifying what it should be shortened to, so Choice (A) is wrong. Choice (C) is wrong because the passage suggests that a shorter workweek could lead to a lower standard of living, not a reduction in the quality of life. Choice (D) is wrong because the passage doesn't make value judgments in comparing countries. Choice (E) is correct but isn't the main idea of the passage.

15. **B, E. Harangues** and **diatribes** are the only two choices that match; both mean something along the lines of lectures or rants. You don't even need to read the sentence. **Discourses** are verbal communications, **homilies** are sermons, **platitudes** are clichés, and **parables** are stories.

16. **B, E.** *Iconoclastic* and *sacrilegious* both describe a disrespectful attitude toward religion or beliefs. *Bombastic* (overbearing), *deleterious* (harmful), *pestilential* (really harmful), and *antagonistic* (hostile) each fit on their own but fail to closely match any of the other words or fit in with the religious theme.

17. **A, B.** The transition word *even* suggests that what the politician or celebrity is called is the opposite of *intelligent*. *Inane* and *fatuous* both mean clueless or dumb. You can instantly rule out *astute* and *perspicacious,* because they mean keen, insightful. You can also rule out *preposterous* and *outlandish,* because they both mean ridiculous, which isn't quite the opposite of intelligent.

18. **D, F.** *Fledglings* and *neophytes* are beginners. *Doyens* and *gurus* wouldn't be just starting out, because they're experts. *Incompetents,* by definition, can't be highly intelligent, and *plebeians* are regular blue-collar folks, which could work if the answer choice had a suitable match.

19. **A, D.** *Lassitude* and *listlessness* suggest low energy, which is what you expect if they're reporting this as a symptom even though they're getting plenty of sleep. *Liquidity* has more to do with financial solvency. *Idleness* is laziness, which conveys a value judgment you wouldn't make about someone depressed. *Melancholy* is unhappiness, and the first part of the sentence establishes that these folks aren't unhappy. *Vivaciousness* (liveliness) is the opposite of what's needed here, so you can rule it out.

20. **C.** The second sentence provides the answer: "one expression of transcendental power, and that is change." Choice (A) is close, but it goes too far in suggesting that the power of sacred cities and cosmic shrines is what causes the changes we observe around us.

Section 4: Quantitative Reasoning

1. **B.** Quantity B equals (100)(100), which can become $\sqrt{(100)(100)(100)(100)}$. Square both sides to lose the radicals, and take a quick average of the numbers in Quantity A, which is less than 100; the numbers in Quantity B average to 100, so Quantity B is greater.

2. **A.** If $n > p$, then $n \therefore p$, or $\dfrac{n}{p+n}$, will always be greater than 0.5 regardless of what numbers are used. Try numbers for n and p that are close together, such as 10 and 9, and numbers that are far apart, such as 10 and 1. As long as $n > p$, the outcome is greater than 0.5.

3. **B.** Use the combinations formula for this one:

$$_nC_r = \frac{n!}{r!(n-r)!}$$

If $n = 10$ members and they're choosing $r = 3$ representatives, then

$$\frac{10!}{3! \times 7!} = \frac{10 \times 9 \times 8 \times 7!}{3! \times 7!} = \frac{10 \times 9 \times 8}{3 \times 2 \times 1} = \frac{720}{6} = 120$$

4. **C.** To get a 1.5% solution, mix equal parts of a 1.0% and a 2.0% solution. To prove this, create an equation by picking 1 for the parts of 1.0% solution, setting x as the number of parts of 2.0% solution, and $(x+1)$ as the combined amount of 1.5% solution. Set the equation up like this:

$$(1)(1.0\%) + (x)(2.0\%) = (x+1)(1.5\%)$$

Then solve for x.

5. **A.** If the square's area is 16, then each side is 4, giving the circle a diameter of 4 and a radius of 2. The area of the circle, using πr^2, is 4π. Place this value over the area of the square, 16, and reduce the fraction to $\frac{\pi}{4}$. This is the fraction of the circle covered by the square. Because π is slightly greater than 3, Quantity A is greater.

6. **C.** The cube of volume 8 has each side equal to 2. On one face of the cube, connect the corners to create a 45-45-90 triangle. Because each side of the triangle is 2, the hypotenuse of this triangle is $2\sqrt{2}$.

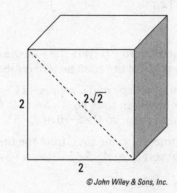
© John Wiley & Sons, Inc.

Now, to find the distance between the opposite corners farthest apart on the cube, create a new right triangle with the hypotenuse of the first right triangle (the 45-45-90 triangle from before) as the base, one side of the cube as the height, and the target line, which represents the distance between the two farthest points, as the hypotenuse:

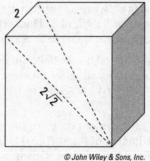
© John Wiley & Sons, Inc.

It helps to draw the new triangle outside the cube:

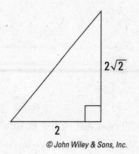
© John Wiley & Sons, Inc.

The base is 2 (from the side of the cube), and the height is $2\sqrt{2}$ (from the hypotenuse of the first triangle added). Use the Pythagorean theorem to find the hypotenuse of the new triangle:

$$2^2 + \left(2\sqrt{2}\right)^2 = c^2$$
$$4 + 8 = c^2$$
$$c = \sqrt{12}$$
$$= \sqrt{2 \times 2 \times 3}$$
$$= 2\sqrt{3}$$

7. **C.** The angle supplementary to y (inside the triangle) can be written as $180 - y$ or $180 - 2x$ because it's the third angle of the triangle. Therefore, y equals $2x$.

8. **A.** Let A represent Andrew's age and C represent Carl's age. Write out the two equations: Andrew is five years older than Carl, so $A - 5 = C$. In five years, Carl's age will be 20% less than (or 80% of) Andrew's age, so $C + 5 = 0.8(A + 5)$.

   To solve for A, substitute the value for C from the first equation for the value of C in the second equation. Now you have $A - 5 + 5 = 0.8(A + 5)$. Solve for A:

   $$A - 5 + 5 = 0.8A + 4$$
   $$A = 0.8A + 4$$
   $$0.2A = 4$$
   $$A = 20$$

   The quantities are not equal, because Quantity A represents Andrew's age in five years, which is 25.

9. **E.** The volume of a cube is e^3, where e represents an edge, so back solve the cube with a volume of 27 to find the edge length of 3. The surface area is the sum of the areas of each face. Because each edge is 3, each face is 9. Six faces give the cube a surface area of 54.

10. **A.** Because the employee added a new ball, the number of balls in the machine is $n + 1$, which is also the number of possibilities for the first ball selected. The numbers of possibilities for the second and third balls selected are n and $n - 1$, respectively. Multiply these together for $n(n^2 - 1)$.

11. **D.** Draw a line from Point P straight down to the x-axis. Now you have a right triangle. Because the (x, y) coordinates of Point P are $\left(1, \sqrt{3}\right)$ respectively, these coordinates are also the base and height of the triangle. This is a 30-60-90 triangle with side ratios of $1 : 2 : \sqrt{3}$, making the hypotenuse, and the distance of Point P from the origin, equal to 2.

    If you don't know that the side ratios of a 30-60-90 triangle are $1 : 2 : \sqrt{3}$, you can use the Pythagorean theorem to calculate the length of the hypotenuse:

    $$a^2 + b^2 = c^2$$
    $$1^2 + \sqrt{3}^2 = c^2$$
    $$1 + 3 = c^2$$
    $$4 = c^2$$
    $$c = 2$$

12. **D.** If 15 kWh represents 30 percent of the family's total daily electricity usage, the total daily usage would be $0.30x = 15$ kWh; $x = \dfrac{15}{0.30} = 50$ kWh per day. At \$0.15 per kWh in the northeast, that's a daily cost of \$7.50. Multiply \$7.50 by 365 days for an annual electricity cost of \$2,737.50, or approximately \$2,700.

13. **A.** In this problem, $4,500 represents the family's total electric bill. Heating alone represents 30% of that, or $4,500 times 0.30, which equals $1,350. Cutting the heating bill by 35% saves them $1,350 times 0.35, which is $472.50, which is pretty close to $500 per year in savings. And $8,000 divided by $500 is 16 years; actually, the number of years to recoup the investment is somewhat more than that due to rounding $472.50 up to $500.

14. **A.** Assume a total usage of 100 kWh per day; therefore, it takes 30%, or 30 kWh, to heat a home and 20%, or 20 kWh, to cool it per day. The cost of cooling a home in the northeast is 20 kWh times $0.15, which is $3. The cost of heating a home in the northwest is 30 kWh times $0.07, which is $2.10 per day. The second answer is wrong, because $(75 \times 0.10 \times 365) - (50 \times 0.10 \times 365) = \$912.50$. The third answer is wrong, because moving from the northeast to the south central region results in a savings of $0.15 - \$0.09 = \$0.06$ per kWh, which translates into a daily savings of $50 \text{ kWh} \times \$0.06 = \$3.00$ per day, which translates into $3 per day for 365 days per year, or $1,095, and 30% of that is $328.50.

15. **1.** Factor the numerator to reduce the fraction, like this:

$$\frac{2^{11} - 2^{10}}{2^{10}} = \frac{2^{10}(2-1)}{2^{10}} = (2-1) = 1$$

16. **3.** Add up the digits: $2+1+0+4+2+3 = 12$. Because 12 is divisible by 3, the entire number is divisible by 3. The only prime number smaller than 3 is 2, but because 210,423 is an odd number, it won't factor into 2.

17. **220.** Use the combinations formula to solve this one:

$$_nC_r = \frac{n!}{r!(n-r)!}$$

If $n = 12$ students and they're choosing $r = 3$ representatives, then the number of combinations is

$$\frac{12!}{3! \times (12-3)!} = \frac{12!}{3! \times 9!} = \frac{12 \times 11 \times 10 \times 9!}{3! \times 9!} = \frac{12 \times 11 \times 10}{3 \times 2 \times 1} = \frac{1,320}{6} = 220$$

18. **A, C.** The *range* refers to the distance between the lowest and highest numbers in the set and can be found by subtracting the lowest number from the highest number. If the new integer x brings the range to 8, then x must either be –1 or 11. If x is –1, the new average is 4; if it's 11, the new average is 6.

19. **A, E.** Using the formula for the area of a cylinder, $\pi r^2 h$, substitute 4 for h and try integers for r until the volume equals or surpasses 20π, the highest answer choice. With r values of 1, 2, and 3, the volumes of the cylinder are 4π, 16π, and 36π, respectively.

20. **A, C.** The first choice is correct, because the lowest value of xy must be $48\,(6 \times 8)$, and any higher value must be a multiple of 48, making it also a multiple of 24. You can rule out the second choice, because if xy were 48, then xy divided by 16 would be the odd number 3. However, xy isn't limited to 48; it could also be 96 or 144, just to name a couple of options. These other values wouldn't produce odd numbers if divided by 16. The last choice is also correct, because if y is a multiple of 12, then it has at least one 3 as a factor. Therefore, the numerator $3y$ has at least two 3s as factors (one each from the 3 and the y), which cancel with the denominator 9, regardless of which multiple of $12y$ is.

Answer Key for Practice Exam 1

Section 1: Verbal Reasoning	Section 2: Quantitative Reasoning	Section 3: Verbal Reasoning	Section 4: Quantitative Reasoning
1. B	1. B	1. E	1. B
2. D	2. C	2. B	2. A
3. A, E	3. C	3. D	3. B
4. C, D	4. A	4. A, D	4. C
5. A, E	5. C	5. B, F	5. A
6. C, D, H	6. B	6. C, F, H	6. C
7. C, E, G	7. C	7. A, E, I	7. C
8. A	8. C	8. D	8. A
9. C	9. D	9. A, B	9. E
10. C	10. D	10. D	10. A
11. E	11. A	11. B	11. D
12. E	12. B	12. D	12. D
13. B	13. A	13. C	13. A
14. D	14. C	14. B	14. A
15. A, B, C	15. 2	15. B, E	15. 1
16. B, E	16. $18,500	16. B, E	16. 3
17. B, E	17. 22	17. A, B	17. 220
18. A, F	18. A, C	18. D, F	18. A, C
19. C, D	19. A, C, E	19. A, D	19. A, E
20. B, F	20. B, C, D	20. C	20. A, C

Chapter 6

Practice Exam 2

• •

*L*ike the actual, computer-based GRE, the following exam consists of two 30-minute essays, two 30-minute Verbal Reasoning sections (20 questions each), and two 35-minute Quantitative Reasoning sections (20 questions each). The actual GRE may also include an extra Verbal or Quantitative Reasoning section, which doesn't count toward your score, but this practice exam has nothing like that.

Take this practice test under normal exam conditions and approach it as you would the real GRE:

- ✔ **Work when you won't be interrupted.** If you have to, lock yourself in your room or go to the library so your housemates won't disturb you. And turn off your cellphone.

- ✔ **Use scratch paper that's free of any prepared notes.** On the actual GRE, you receive blank scratch paper before your test begins.

- ✔ **Answer as many questions as time allows.** Consider answering all the easier questions within each section first and then going back to answer the remaining, harder questions. Because you're not penalized for guessing, go ahead and guess on the remaining questions before time expires.

- ✔ **Set a timer for each section.** If you have time left at the end, you may go back and review answers (within the section), continue and finish your test early, or pause and catch your mental breath before moving on to the next section.

- ✔ **Don't leave your desk while the clock is running on any section.** Though technically you're allowed to do this, it's not conducive to an effective time-management strategy.

- ✔ **Take breaks between sections.** Take a one-minute break after each section and the optional ten-minute break after the first Verbal section.

- ✔ **Type the essays.** Because you type the essays on the actual GRE, typing them now is good practice. Don't use software, such as Microsoft Word, with automatic spell-checker or other formatting features. Instead, use a simple text editor, such as Notepad, with copy and paste but no other features. The GRE essay-writing field features undo, redo, copy, and paste functionality but nothing else.

After completing this entire practice test, go to Chapter 7 to check your answers. Be sure to review the explanations for *all* the questions, not just the ones you miss. The answer explanations provide insight and a review of various concepts. This way, too, you review the explanations for questions that you guessed correctly on.

Chances are good that you'll be taking the computerized GRE, which doesn't have answer choices marked with A, B, C, D, E, and F. Instead, you'll see clickable ovals and check boxes, fill-in-the-blank text boxes, and click-a-sentence options (in some Reading Comprehension questions). I formatted the questions and answer choices to make them appear as similar as possible to what you'll see on the computer-based test, but I had to retain the A, B, C, D, E, F choices for marking your answers.

Answer Sheet for Practice Exam 2

Section 1:
Verbal Reasoning

1. Ⓐ Ⓑ Ⓒ Ⓓ Ⓔ
2. Ⓐ Ⓑ Ⓒ Ⓓ Ⓔ
3. Ⓐ Ⓑ Ⓒ Ⓓ Ⓔ Ⓕ
4. Ⓐ Ⓑ Ⓒ Ⓓ Ⓔ Ⓕ
5. Ⓐ Ⓑ Ⓒ Ⓓ Ⓔ Ⓕ
6. Ⓐ Ⓑ Ⓒ Ⓓ Ⓔ Ⓕ Ⓖ Ⓗ Ⓘ
7. Ⓐ Ⓑ Ⓒ Ⓓ Ⓔ Ⓕ Ⓖ Ⓗ Ⓘ
8. Ⓐ Ⓑ Ⓒ Ⓓ Ⓔ
9. Ａ Ｂ Ｃ
10. Ⓐ Ⓑ Ⓒ Ⓓ Ⓔ
11. Ⓐ Ⓑ Ⓒ Ⓓ Ⓔ
12. Ａ Ｂ Ｃ
13. Ⓐ Ⓑ Ⓒ Ⓓ Ⓔ
14. Ａ Ｂ Ｃ
15. Ａ Ｂ Ｃ Ｄ Ｅ Ｆ
16. Ａ Ｂ Ｃ Ｄ Ｅ Ｆ
17. Ａ Ｂ Ｃ Ｄ Ｅ Ｆ
18. Ａ Ｂ Ｃ Ｄ Ｅ Ｆ
19. Ａ Ｂ Ｃ Ｄ Ｅ Ｆ
20. Ⓐ Ⓑ Ⓒ Ⓓ Ⓔ

Section 2:
Quantitative Reasoning

1. Ⓐ Ⓑ Ⓒ Ⓓ
2. Ⓐ Ⓑ Ⓒ Ⓓ
3. Ⓐ Ⓑ Ⓒ Ⓓ
4. Ⓐ Ⓑ Ⓒ Ⓓ
5. Ⓐ Ⓑ Ⓒ Ⓓ
6. Ⓐ Ⓑ Ⓒ Ⓓ Ⓔ
7. Ⓐ Ⓑ Ⓒ Ⓓ Ⓔ
8. $ [,   ]
9. Ⓐ Ⓑ Ⓒ Ⓓ Ⓔ
10. Ａ Ｂ Ｃ Ｄ
11. Ⓐ Ⓑ Ⓒ Ⓓ Ⓔ
12. Ａ Ｂ Ｃ Ｄ
13. Ⓐ Ⓑ Ⓒ Ⓓ Ⓔ
14. Ⓐ Ⓑ Ⓒ Ⓓ Ⓔ
15. [:   ]
16. Ⓐ Ⓑ Ⓒ Ⓓ Ⓔ
17. Ⓐ Ⓑ Ⓒ Ⓓ Ⓔ
18. [   ]
19. Ａ Ｂ Ｃ Ｄ Ｅ
20. Ⓐ Ⓑ Ⓒ Ⓓ Ⓔ

Section 3:
Verbal Reasoning

1. Ⓐ Ⓑ Ⓒ Ⓓ Ⓔ
2. Ⓐ Ⓑ Ⓒ Ⓓ Ⓔ
3. Ⓐ Ⓑ Ⓒ Ⓓ Ⓔ Ⓕ
4. Ⓐ Ⓑ Ⓒ Ⓓ Ⓔ Ⓕ
5. Ⓐ Ⓑ Ⓒ Ⓓ Ⓔ Ⓕ
6. Ⓐ Ⓑ Ⓒ Ⓓ Ⓔ Ⓕ Ⓖ Ⓗ Ⓘ
7. Ⓐ Ⓑ Ⓒ Ⓓ Ⓔ Ⓕ Ⓖ Ⓗ Ⓘ
8. Ⓐ Ⓑ Ⓒ Ⓓ Ⓔ
9. Ａ Ｂ Ｃ
10. Ⓐ Ⓑ Ⓒ Ⓓ Ⓔ
11. Ⓐ Ⓑ Ⓒ Ⓓ Ⓔ
12. Ａ Ｂ Ｃ
13. Ⓐ Ⓑ Ⓒ Ⓓ Ⓔ
14. Ⓐ Ⓑ Ⓒ Ⓓ Ⓔ
15. Ａ Ｂ Ｃ Ｄ Ｅ Ｆ
16. Ａ Ｂ Ｃ Ｄ Ｅ Ｆ
17. Ａ Ｂ Ｃ Ｄ Ｅ Ｆ
18. Ａ Ｂ Ｃ Ｄ Ｅ Ｆ
19. Ａ Ｂ Ｃ Ｄ Ｅ Ｆ
20. Ⓐ Ⓑ Ⓒ Ⓓ Ⓔ

Section 4:
Quantitative Reasoning

1. Ⓐ Ⓑ Ⓒ Ⓓ
2. Ⓐ Ⓑ Ⓒ Ⓓ
3. Ⓐ Ⓑ Ⓒ Ⓓ
4. Ⓐ Ⓑ Ⓒ Ⓓ
5. Ⓐ Ⓑ Ⓒ Ⓓ
6. Ⓐ Ⓑ Ⓒ Ⓓ
7. Ⓐ Ⓑ Ⓒ Ⓓ
8. Ⓐ Ⓑ Ⓒ Ⓓ
9. Ⓐ Ⓑ Ⓒ Ⓓ Ⓔ
10. Ⓐ Ⓑ Ⓒ Ⓓ Ⓔ
11. Ⓐ Ⓑ Ⓒ Ⓓ Ⓔ
12. $ [,   ]
13. Ⓐ Ⓑ Ⓒ Ⓓ Ⓔ
14. Ⓐ Ⓑ Ⓒ Ⓓ Ⓔ
15. Ⓐ Ⓑ Ⓒ Ⓓ Ⓔ
16. Ａ Ｂ Ｃ Ｄ Ｅ
17. Ⓐ Ⓑ Ⓒ Ⓓ Ⓔ
18. Ⓐ Ⓑ Ⓒ Ⓓ Ⓔ
19. Ⓐ Ⓑ Ⓒ Ⓓ Ⓔ
20. Ａ Ｂ Ｃ

Analytical Writing 1: Analyze an Issue

Time: 30 minutes

"Freedom of speech should provide students the right to say or write anything they wish in class or class assignments, as long as it is not slanderous or libelous."

Directions: Discuss the extent to which you agree or disagree with the previous statement, and explain your reasoning for the position you take. In developing and supporting your position, you should consider ways in which the statement may or may not hold true and explain how those considerations shape your position.

Analytical Writing 2: Analyze an Argument

Time: 30 minutes

The following appeared in a letter to the editor of the *Flint Herald* newspaper.

"Globalization is the best solution to poverty, giving even the poorest countries access to markets and opportunities anywhere in the world. Statistics show that as world economies have become more globalized, poverty has declined. According to the Global Poverty Report, the proportion of the world's population living in poverty declined from 29% in 1988 to 26% in 1998. The World Bank reports that the number of people living below the international poverty line of $1.25 per day fell from 1.8 billion to 1.4 billion between 1990 and 2005."

Directions: Write a response in which you examine the unstated assumptions of the previous argument. Be sure to explain how the argument depends on the assumptions and what the implications are if the assumptions prove unwarranted.

STOP DO NOT TURN THE PAGE UNTIL TOLD TO DO SO.
DO NOT RETURN TO A PREVIOUS TEST.

Section 1

Verbal Reasoning

Time: 30 minutes for 20 questions

Directions: Choose the best answer to each question. Blacken the corresponding oval(s) on the answer sheet.

Directions: For Questions 1–7, choose the one entry best suited for each blank from its corresponding column of choices.

1. The _____ aim of the new bill was to cut spending. When the bill was passed, citizens were surprised to learn that the spending "cuts" were merely reductions in future spending increases.

A explicit
B primary
C fundamental
D ostensible
E incipient

2. The administration's refusal to divest itself of the oil industry is one of the best examples of _____ that student activists have observed. The administration's argument seems plausible, but in glossing over the political impact that divestiture tends to have on future outcomes, the argument belies the administration's penchant to deceive.

A sophistry
B dogmatism
C bias
D probity
E glasnost

3. The author's account of the incident was far too (i) _____. It would have been more compelling had he (ii) _____ it.

Blank (i)	Blank (ii)
A devious	D encapsulated
B elaborate	E expanded
C spurious	F embellished

4. With the growing popularity of social media, online (i) _____ is becoming ubiquitous. Even though experts constantly warn users against engaging in verbal battles online, even those users who exhibit (ii) _____ in face-to-face encounters are frequently drawn unwittingly into heated online debates.

Blank (i)	Blank (ii)
A enmity	D discomfiture
B pretense	E effrontery
C vitriol	F aplomb

5. Because neither solution was (i) _____, the committee had to schedule additional meetings to consider other options that were more (ii) _____.

Blank (i)	Blank (ii)
A verifiable	D plausible
B standard	E feasible
C viable	F probable

Go on to next page

6. Without (i) _____ data to back up the researcher's claims, most experts found the report's conclusions (ii) _____ at best and perhaps even (iii) _____.

Blank (i)	Blank (ii)	Blank (iii)
Ⓐ speculative	Ⓓ conceivable	Ⓖ certain
Ⓑ empirical	Ⓔ convincing	Ⓗ ascertainable
Ⓒ scholarly	Ⓕ dubious	Ⓘ fraudulent

7. The king's plan was (i) _____. His country's offerings of financial assistance for economic development and humanitarian aid seemed quite (ii) _____, but this generosity was motivated by a desire to (iii) _____ the host country with spies and other operatives.

Blank (i)	Blank (ii)	Blank (iii)
Ⓐ insidious	Ⓓ pedestrian	Ⓖ infiltrate
Ⓑ innocuous	Ⓔ miserly	Ⓗ inoculate
Ⓒ vindictive	Ⓕ magnanimous	Ⓘ obviate

Directions: Each of the following passages is followed by questions pertaining to the passage. Read the passage and answer the questions based on information stated or implied in that passage. For each question, select one answer choice unless instructed otherwise.

The concept of growing fuel to power our cars seems like a good idea in countries where food is plentiful, but in countries where food is scarce, this practice is considered criminal. It comes down to a choice of whether to eat or drive. According to the World Bank, 33 countries may face unrest because of surging food costs and deepening poverty as food supplies dwindle and prices rise. Developed nations with surplus yields must take note soon and stop the development of biofuels.

8. Which of the following, if true, most effectively undermines the argument that nations must stop the development of biofuels?

    Ⓐ Biofuels can be developed from non-food crops, such as jatropha, an oilseed-bearing tree.

    Ⓑ As oil supplies dwindle, we have no other choice but to convert foodstuffs into fuel.

    Ⓒ Nations use only their surplus crops for use in producing biofuels.

    Ⓓ Biofuels can be developed from waste products that would otherwise be discarded, such as wood waste and parts of plants not used to feed people.

    Ⓔ Biofuels are more environmentally friendly than fossil fuels, including coal and oil.

The following passage is taken from A History of Modern Africa: 1800 to the Present, *by Richard Reid (Wiley-Blackwell).*

Historians of Africa have made use of a range of sources. The identification of usable sources was particularly important for the precolonial past, as few societies — with the exception of the Arabic north and the Ethiopian highlands — left behind written records. Archeology was used to chart material and cultural change over the longer term, while linguistic change and spread could also be employed in discerning social, economic, and political metamorphosis. Historians have also had to make use of the written sources of foreigners, beginning with those of the Arabic-speaking travelers and traders from the Middle Ages onward, and after the sixteenth century those of European missionaries, traders, and explorers; in the twentieth century, extensive use of a vast array of colonial records has supported new avenues of historical research. Yet scholars have also been able to utilize the recorded indigenous oral histories and traditions which are the heart of all communities, and the testimonies which have been recorded in the course of the twentieth century. Clearly, each of these types of sources has its limitations as well as its contribution to make. Studies of archeology and language generally permit the historian to glimpse only very approximate timescales, and only very broad patterns of change; the written words of foreigners are

Go on to next page

riddled with the cultural and social prejudices and misunderstandings characteristic of outsiders, though some are more problematic and insensitive than others. Indigenous oral histories themselves were prone to change and distortion over time, and as a general rule favoured the authors' particular lineage as well as reflecting current political circumstances. Nonetheless, used with caution, these sources have proved invaluable, and their utilization in the 1950s and 1960s reflected a new respect for (and indeed empathy with) Africa's past.

For Question 9, consider each answer choice separately and select all answer choices that are correct.

9. Based on the passage, early sources of African history have which of the following limitations?

    A   Written records of foreigners are influenced by cultural and social prejudices.

    B   Archeology and language studies may not provide specific dates.

    C   Arabic-speaking travelers kept no written records.

10. One could reasonably infer from this passage that the greatest challenge for African historians is

    Ⓐ finding sufficient historical resources.

    Ⓑ discovering recorded indigenous oral histories.

    Ⓒ locating indigenous populations that know African history.

    Ⓓ discerning which sources of historical data are reliable and which are not.

    Ⓔ gaining access to archeological sites.

Colleges give far too much weight to standardized test scores. After all, a standardized test does not measure a student's innate ability; it only measures how well prepared the student is to take the test. Students attending college preparatory and other premier high schools have a distinct and unfair advantage, because teachers at these schools tend to teach to the test, and parents are willing to pay for coaching and materials designed to help boost test scores.

11. Which of the following, if true, most seriously counters the argument that standardized test scores reflect more on students' academic advantages than their academic performance?

    Ⓐ Studies show that students who score higher on the SAT earn more regardless of the college they attend.

    Ⓑ Students who score lower on standardized tests often become so discouraged they do not even apply for college.

    Ⓒ Standardized test scores show how well different school systems prepare students for college.

    Ⓓ Studies show that students who score lower on the SAT experience a significantly higher dropout rate.

    Ⓔ Several other factors contribute in accurately predicting a student's college success, including grades, community service, and work ethic.

The following passage is taken from The Immortality Edge: Realize the Secrets of Your Telomeres for a Longer, Healthier Life, *by Michael Fossel, Greta Blackburn, and Dave Woynarowski (Wiley).*

Until now, the concept of immortality was considered forever unachievable. Over time, the cells in our bodies reach a stage at which they can no longer reproduce themselves — a retirement-like state in which they die or no longer divide and thus become inert. This end point is called senescence. The effect of senescent cells appears obviously when they accumulate in quite large numbers in just one tissue (the cartilage in our joints), but even in small numbers they pose a disproportionate, although less obvious, threat to the surrounding healthy tissues because of their steadily deteriorating metabolic state.

Go on to next page

For Question 12, consider each answer choice separately and select **all** answer choices that are correct.

12. The following are characteristics of senescent cells:

    A. Cartilaginous

    B. Inability to reproduce

    C. Deteriorating metabolic state

The following passage is taken from All You Have to Do Is Listen: Music from the Inside Out, by Rob Kapilow (Wiley).

In *Understanding Media,* Marshall McLuhan discusses a famous acting exercise in which the great theater director Stanislavsky used to ask his young actors to pronounce and stress the word "tonight" fifty different ways while the audience wrote down the different shades of meaning expressed. Though an actor may be able to express fifty different shades of feeling and meaning using tone, pitch, volume, accentuation, and facial and body gestures when he says the word out loud, the written word for all of them is the same — t-o-n-i-g-h-t. As McLuhan points out, the written word takes this rich web of dramatic meaning, removes its aural subtleties and nuances, and abstracts it into a single, cool, visual, symbolic representation — the phonetic word. Though we casually consider the written and spoken forms of the word to be identical twins, they are really distant cousins. If the written word wants to convey all the rich meanings contained in the spoken version, it must spell them out one by one.

13. Which sentence best summarizes the passage?

    Ⓐ In *Understanding Media,* Marshall McLuhan discusses a famous acting exercise in which the great theater director Stanislavsky used to ask his young actors to pronounce and stress the word "tonight" fifty different ways while the audience wrote down the different shades of meaning expressed.

    Ⓑ Though an actor may be able to express fifty different shades of feeling and meaning using tone, pitch, volume, accentuation, and facial and body gestures when he says the word out loud, the written word for all of them is the same — t-o-n-i-g-h-t.

    Ⓒ As McLuhan points out, the written word takes this rich web of dramatic meaning, removes its aural subtleties and nuances, and abstracts it into a single, cool, visual, symbolic representation — the phonetic word.

    Ⓓ Though we casually consider the written and spoken forms of the word to be identical twins, they are really distant cousins.

    Ⓔ If the written word wants to convey all the rich meanings contained in the spoken version, it must spell them out one by one.

For Question 14, consider each answer choice separately and select **all** answer choices that are correct.

14. According to the passage, an actor can alter the meaning of a word by using which of the following?

    A. Gestures

    B. Rhythm

    C. Resonance

Go on to next page

Directions: Each of the following sentences has a blank indicating that a word or phrase is omitted. Choose the two answer choices that best complete the sentence and result in two sentences most alike in meaning.

15. The professor's _____ speech, intended to impress his colleagues, served only to prove how pretentious he really was.

    A austere

    B pedantic

    C sonorous

    D pusillanimous

    E bombastic

    F ravenous

16. The filter was far too _____ and failed to adequately remove the impurities.

    A absorbent

    B resistant

    C dissolute

    D porous

    E dilatory

    F permeable

17. Unrelenting storm waves battered the ship for days, causing intense damage to the ship and _____ the passengers and crew.

    A exhausting

    B inflicting

    C enervating

    D ameliorating

    E castigating

    F energizing

18. The _____ senators voted along party lines for the bill, refusing to consider the amendments made to address their objections.

    A independent

    B tendentious

    C insipid

    D duplicitous

    E stubborn

    F partisan

19. In the United States, people tend to _____ celebrities, while people from other countries tend to be less impressed by celebrity status.

    A embellish

    B disparage

    C venerate

    D eschew

    E aggrandize

    F proclaim

Read the passage and answer the question based on information stated or implied in the passage.

This passage is taken from The Little Book of Economics: How the Economy Works in the Real World, *by Greg Ip (Wiley).*

Numerous factors determine a country's success and whether its companies are good investments. Inflation and interest rates, consumer spending, and business confidence are important in the short run. In the long run, though, a country becomes rich or stagnates depending on whether it has the right mix of people, capital, and ideas. Get these fundamentals right, and the short-run gyrations seldom matter.

20. Which of the following factors is not mentioned in the passage as contributing to a country's short- or long-term financial success?

    Ⓐ Inflation rate

    Ⓑ Investment capital

    Ⓒ Ideas

    Ⓓ Government spending

    Ⓔ Innovation

STOP DO NOT TURN THE PAGE UNTIL TOLD TO DO SO. DO NOT RETURN TO A PREVIOUS TEST.

Section 2

Quantitative Reasoning

Time: 35 minutes for 20 questions

Notes:

↝ All numbers used in this exam are real numbers.

↝ All figures lie in a plane.

↝ Angle measures are positive; points and angles are in the position shown.

Directions: For Questions 1–5, choose from the following answer choices:

Ⓐ *Quantity A is greater.*

Ⓑ *Quantity B is greater.*

Ⓒ *The two quantities are equal.*

Ⓓ *The relationship cannot be determined from the information given.*

1. *a* is an integer greater than 0.

Quantity A	**Quantity B**
$\left(\dfrac{1}{2a}\right)^2$	$\dfrac{1}{2a^2}$

2. $0 > a > b > c$

Quantity A	**Quantity B**
$a - c$	$a + b$

3.

© John Wiley & Sons, Inc.

Quantity A	**Quantity B**
Area of the triangle	$25\sqrt{3}$

4. $16a + 5b = 37;\ \ 3b - 8a = -21$

Quantity A	**Quantity B**
$a + b$	2

5.

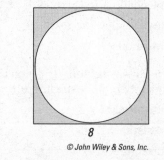

8

© John Wiley & Sons, Inc.

The circle is inscribed within the square.

Quantity A	**Quantity B**
The area of the square not covered by the circle	20

6.

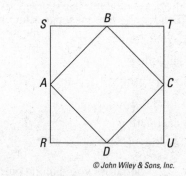

© John Wiley & Sons, Inc.

Square *RSTU* has a perimeter of 48. If *A*, *B*, *C*, and *D* are the midpoints of their respective sides, what is the perimeter of square *ABCD*?

Ⓐ 32

Ⓑ $24\sqrt{2}$

Ⓒ 24

Ⓓ $12\sqrt{3}$

Ⓔ $12\sqrt{2}$

Go on to next page

7. Gigi and Neville, working together at the same rate, can mow the estate's lawn in 12 hours. Working alone, what fraction of the lawn can Gigi mow in three hours?

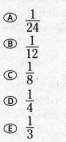

Ⓐ $\frac{1}{24}$

Ⓑ $\frac{1}{12}$

Ⓒ $\frac{1}{8}$

Ⓓ $\frac{1}{4}$

Ⓔ $\frac{1}{3}$

Questions 8–10 are based on the following graphs.

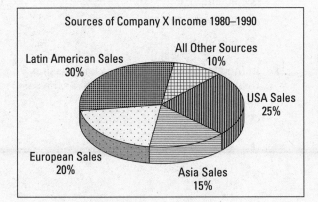

Sources of Company X Income 1980–1990

All Other Sources 10%

Latin American Sales 30%

USA Sales 25%

European Sales 20%

Asia Sales 15%

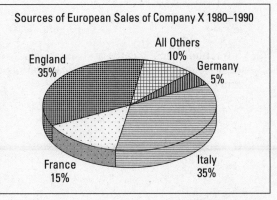

Sources of European Sales of Company X 1980–1990

All Others 10%

England 35%

Germany 5%

France 15%

Italy 35%

© John Wiley & Sons, Inc.

Note: Graphs drawn to scale.

8. If Company X received $50,000 in Latin American Sales from 1980 through 1990, how much money did it receive from sales to France?

Give your answer to the nearest thousand.

$ [,   ]

9. From the information given, the 1985 sales to England were what percent of the sales to Europe?

Ⓐ 100

Ⓑ 50

Ⓒ 35

Ⓓ 25

Ⓔ It cannot be determined.

10. From the information given, sales to France accounted for which of the following in European sales?

Select <u>two</u> answer choices.

Ⓐ Half as much as sales to Italy and Germany combined

Ⓑ Sales to either Italy or England minus 20% of total European sales

Ⓒ Sales to England minus 20% of total European sales and sales to Germany plus 10% of total European sales

Ⓓ More than half as much as sales to Italy

Go on to next page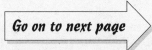

11. If $x \neq -1$ or 0 and $y = \dfrac{1}{x}$, then
    $\dfrac{1}{(x+1)} + \dfrac{1}{(y+1)} =$

    Ⓐ 1

    Ⓑ 3

    Ⓒ x

    Ⓓ $x+1$

    Ⓔ $\dfrac{(x+1)}{(x+2)}$

12. If $5(x+2)^2 - 125 = 0$, then $x =$
    Select <u>two</u> answer choices.

    Ⓐ 3

    Ⓑ –3

    Ⓒ –7

    Ⓓ 25

13. If ten plums cost a cents and six apples cost b cents, what is the cost of two plums and two apples in terms of a and b?

    Ⓐ $\dfrac{3a+5b}{15}$

    Ⓑ $3a + 5b$

    Ⓒ $15ab$

    Ⓓ $5a + \dfrac{3b}{15}$

    Ⓔ $\dfrac{1}{15ab}$

14. If $x \neq 4$, which of the following is equivalent to $\left(\dfrac{\sqrt{x}+2}{\sqrt{x}-2} \right)^{-1}$?

    Ⓐ –1

    Ⓑ $\dfrac{x+4}{x-4}$

    Ⓒ $-\sqrt{x}-1$

    Ⓓ $\sqrt{x}+4$

    Ⓔ $\dfrac{\sqrt{x}-2}{\sqrt{x}+2}$

15. Each of two right circular cylinders has a height of 10. Cylinder A has a circumference of 10π. Cylinder B has a circumference of 20π. What is the ratio of the volume of Cylinder A to the volume of Cylinder B?

16. A plane flies from Los Angeles to New York at 600 miles per hour and returns along the same route at 400 miles per hour. What is the average (arithmetic mean) flying speed for the entire route?

    Ⓐ 460 mph

    Ⓑ 480 mph

    Ⓒ 500 mph

    Ⓓ 540 mph

    Ⓔ 560 mph

17. In the xy-coordinate plane, a line passing through the points (3, 2) and (8, 14) has a slope of

    Ⓐ $\dfrac{5}{12}$

    Ⓑ $\dfrac{3}{2}$

    Ⓒ $\dfrac{11}{6}$

    Ⓓ $\dfrac{12}{5}$

    Ⓔ $\dfrac{21}{5}$

18. If a is the smallest prime number greater than 3 and b is the largest prime number less than 11, then what is the value of ab?

Go on to next page ➡

19. $|x| > 17$

    Which of the following integers makes the preceding equation true?

    Select all the correct answers.

    A −21
    B 15
    C −15
    D 20
    E −32

20. $7x + 4y = 53$

    $9x − 4y = −5$

    Given the preceding equations, what is the value of xy?

    Ⓐ −69
    Ⓑ −24
    Ⓒ 16
    Ⓓ −16
    Ⓔ 24

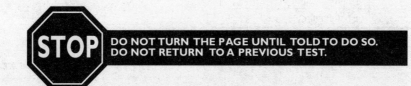

STOP DO NOT TURN THE PAGE UNTIL TOLD TO DO SO.
DO NOT RETURN TO A PREVIOUS TEST.

Section 3

Verbal Reasoning

Time: 30 minutes for 20 questions

Directions: Choose the best answer to each question. Blacken the corresponding oval(s) on the answer sheet.

Directions: For Questions 1–7, choose the one entry best suited for each blank from its corresponding column of choices.

1. The release of classified documents triggered a diplomatic _____ that even the most experienced secretary of state found difficult to address.

Ⓐ coup
Ⓑ dissolution
Ⓒ caucus
Ⓓ faux pas
Ⓔ imbroglio

2. Any form of advertising that is not on-demand is considered _____. Potential consumers who do not appreciate being inundated with advertising are more likely to be turned away than drawn in by these intrusive marketing tactics.

Ⓐ abstemious
Ⓑ presumptuous
Ⓒ scurrilous
Ⓓ pusillanimous
Ⓔ contumely

3. Dictators tend to be (i) _____, more skilled at enforcing policies than explaining them. In a democracy, however, elected officials cannot afford to act with such (ii) _____ when dealing with the electorate.

Blank (i)	Blank (ii)
Ⓐ dogmatic	Ⓓ intransigence
Ⓑ acquiescent	Ⓔ diplomacy
Ⓒ libertine	Ⓕ alacrity

4. In high school, Alice was always at the top of her class academically. However, when trying to impress her classmates, she often showed a (i) _____ of knowledge but a (ii) _____ of wisdom.

Blank (i)	Blank (ii)
Ⓐ scarcity	Ⓓ paucity
Ⓑ cache	Ⓔ surplus
Ⓒ plethora	Ⓕ propensity

5. While the president (i) _____ on whether to approve funding for the project, contractors were understandably (ii) _____ of proceeding with construction.

Blank (i)	Blank (ii)
Ⓐ vituperated	Ⓓ wary
Ⓑ vacillated	Ⓔ weary
Ⓒ considered	Ⓕ perfidious

6. Most scholars considered the critic's review (i) _____, merely rehashing (ii) _____ thinking. Expecting something more (iii) _____, they were sorely disappointed.

Blank (i)	Blank (ii)	Blank (iii)
Ⓐ insightful	Ⓓ mandibular	Ⓖ prestigious
Ⓑ banal	Ⓔ conventional	Ⓗ sophisticated
Ⓒ intriguing	Ⓕ secular	Ⓘ tawdry

Go on to next page ➡

7. Despite the (i) _____ of the situation, he remained (ii) _____, revealing his (iii) _____ toward sadness.

Blank (i)	Blank (ii)	Blank (iii)
Ⓐ seriousness	Ⓓ morose	Ⓖ proclivity
Ⓑ urgency	Ⓔ unresponsive	Ⓗ appetite
Ⓒ levity	Ⓕ indifferent	Ⓘ attitude

Directions: Each of the following passages is followed by questions pertaining to the passage. Read the passage and answer the questions based on information stated or implied in that passage. For each question, select one answer choice unless instructed otherwise.

The federal income tax system in the United States is progressive, meaning the more money you earn, the higher your tax rate. Unfortunately, this hits the middle class hardest. People in the lowest income tax bracket pay little to nothing and may even benefit from the earned income tax credit. People in the highest income tax brackets may enjoy tax breaks, because they have access to professionals who can help exploit loopholes and exemptions. This may be considered unfair, because those able to take on more of the tax burden should do so. A viable and fair solution is a flat tax, in which everyone pays the same rate, regardless of earned income, with some exemptions for those earning below a certain amount.

8. Which of the following, if true, most effectively undermines the argument that the flat tax is a fair solution for taxpayers?

Ⓐ The flat tax would simplify tax forms to such an extent that most people in the income tax industry would lose their jobs.

Ⓑ The flat tax would not apply to passive income including capital gains and dividends.

Ⓒ Paying the same rate means those earning the most will pay more than everyone else.

Ⓓ The flat tax will generate more revenue for the federal government.

Ⓔ A national sales tax would be fairer, taxing consumption instead of income.

The following passage is taken from The Paleo Diet: Lose Weight and Get Healthy by Eating the Foods You Were Designed to Eat, *by Loren Cordain (Wiley).*

What do Paleolithic people have to do with us? Actually, quite a lot: DNA evidence shows that basic human physiology has changed little in 40,000 years. Literally, we are Stone Agers living in the Space Age; our dietary needs are the same as theirs. Our genes are well adapted to a world in which all the food eaten daily had to be hunted, fished, or gathered from the natural environment — a world that no longer exists. Nature determined what our bodies needed thousands of years before civilization developed, before people started farming and raising domesticated livestock.

In other words, built into our genes is a blueprint for optimal nutrition — a plan that spells out the foods that make us healthy, lean, and fit. Whether you believe the architect of that blueprint is God, or God acting through evolution by natural selection, or by evolution alone, the end result is the same: We need to give our bodies the foods we were originally designed to eat.

Your car is designed to run on gasoline. When you put diesel fuel into its tank, the results are disastrous for the engine. The same principle is true for us: We are designed to run best on the wild plant and animal foods that all human beings gathered and hunted just 333 generations ago. The staples of today's diet — cereals, dairy products, refined sugars, fatty meats, and salted, processed foods — are like diesel fuel to our bodies' metabolic machinery. These foods clog our engines, make us fat, and cause disease and ill health.

For Question 9, consider each answer choice separately and select all answer choices that are correct.

9. This passage makes the following claims:

Ⓐ Our current dietary staples make us fat.

Ⓑ Our genes are nearly identical to those of our Stone Age ancestors.

Ⓒ All people should be hunters and gatherers.

Go on to next page

10. Which of the following assumptions is not made by the author?

    Ⓐ The human digestive system is comparable to an automobile engine.

    Ⓑ If genes remain the same, so must diet.

    Ⓒ The development of civilization always leads to a degradation of diet.

    Ⓓ The human digestive system is unable to adapt to changes in diet.

    Ⓔ Obesity and ill health are caused by poor diet.

11. Which sentence from the passage best summarizes the passage?

    Ⓐ Actually, quite a lot: DNA evidence shows that basic human physiology has changed little in 40,000 years.

    Ⓑ Our genes are well adapted to a world in which all the food eaten daily had to be hunted, fished, or gathered from the natural environment — a world that no longer exists.

    Ⓒ Nature determined what our bodies needed thousands of years before civilization developed, before people started farming and raising domesticated livestock.

    Ⓓ In other words, built into our genes is a blueprint for optimal nutrition — a plan that spells out the foods that make us healthy, lean, and fit.

    Ⓔ Whether you believe the architect of that blueprint is God, or God acting through evolution by natural selection, or by evolution alone, the end result is the same: We need to give our bodies the foods we were originally designed to eat.

The following passage is taken from What Cinema Is! *by Dudley Andrew (Wiley-Blackwell).*

Without any recording device whatever, Emile Reynaud projected moving images in his theater in 1889. Drawing and painting directly onto glass plates, he fashioned brief snippets of a dozen plates each. Ultimately, he came up with a way to roll the glass plates onto reels and made three sequences of 500 plates each. Luminously colored, these stand as precious early works of animation. Even after 1895, certain <u>audacious</u> "filmmakers" bypassed the camera altogether. In the 1920s, Man Ray exposed and developed photographic paper on which he arranged an array of objects. His Rayographs have generally been displayed in museums alongside standard photographs, as if they were made in the same manner. Man Ray's process has been adapted by numerous experimental film artists — notably Stan Brakhage, who glued moths' wings and other matter onto raw film stock, then printed it for his sublime *Mothlight* (1963).

For Question 12, consider each answer choice separately and select <u>all</u> answer choices that are correct.

12. The passage describes which of the following methods for making a movie without using a video camera?

    Ⓐ Standard photography

    Ⓑ Animation

    Ⓒ Using a movie projector

13. Which of the following titles best describes the passage?

    Ⓐ Filmmakers of the 19th Century

    Ⓑ Is a Camera Essential?

    Ⓒ Beyond Filmmaking

    Ⓓ From Photographs to Moving Pictures

    Ⓔ Moth Wings and Other Snippets

14. In this passage, which of the following is the best synonym for *audacious*?

    Ⓐ Overconfident

    Ⓑ Resolute

    Ⓒ Intrepid

    Ⓓ Impudent

    Ⓔ Pompous

Go on to next page

Directions: *Each of the following sentences has a blank indicating that a word or phrase is omitted. Choose the two answer choices that best complete the sentence and result in two sentences most alike in meaning.*

15. The library received so much money from private donors that the county's contribution seemed _____.

    A indispensable

    B insufficient

    C extraneous

    D superfluous

    E profligate

    F licentious

16. Independent voters overwhelmingly backed the new candidate, _____ her support leading into the primaries.

    A buttressing

    B diminishing

    C undermining

    D bolstering

    E counterbalancing

    F alleviating

17. To keep patrons entertained while waiting in line, the amusement park was looking for _____ employees to take on the personas of a variety of cartoon characters.

    A garrulous

    B diffident

    C gregarious

    D introverted

    E extroverted

    F benevolent

18. When dining out, cultured individuals always follow the rules of _____ so as not to appear uncouth.

    A boorish

    B decorum

    C disrespect

    D decoration

    E decadent

    F etiquette

19. The judge considered the prosecutor's reasoning and theory of the case to be _____ and found the suspect innocent of all charges.

    A fallacious

    B imperfect

    C legitimate

    D facetious

    E fallible

    F delusive

Go on to next page

Read the passage and answer the question based on information stated or implied in the passage.

The general public is overly concerned about the environmental impact of genetically engineered foods. Such foods are actually good for the environment. Crops, for example, can be genetically modified to resist disease and pests, reducing the need for herbicides and pesticides. Genetic engineering can also improve yields, so more food can be grown on less land.

20. Which of the following, if true, most effectively undermines the argument that genetically engineered foods are good for the environment?

Ⓐ The genetic structure of every living organism is complex, and test results focus only on short-term effects.

Ⓑ Swiss researchers have shown that green lacewings, environmentally beneficial predatory insects, died prematurely when fed European corn borers that had eaten genetically modified corn.

Ⓒ Scientists successfully transferred a Brazil nut gene into soybean, only to discover later that people allergic to Brazil nuts were similarly allergic to the transgenic soybean.

Ⓓ Genetically modified foods are fairly new, so scientists know very little about the potential benefits or damage they may cause.

Ⓔ Currently, government regulation of genetically engineered foods is very poor, and producers are not required to label products that contain genetically engineered ingredients.

Section 4
Quantitative Reasoning

Time: 35 minutes for 20 questions

Notes:

✔ All numbers used in this exam are real numbers.

✔ All figures lie in a plane.

✔ Angle measures are positive; points and angles are in the position shown.

Directions: For Questions 1–8, choose from the following answer choices:

Ⓐ *Quantity A is greater.*

Ⓑ *Quantity B is greater.*

Ⓒ *The two quantities are equal.*

Ⓓ *The relationship cannot be determined from the information given.*

1.

Quantity A	Quantity B
Area of a rectangle of perimeter 20	Area of a triangle of perimeter 20

2. $a \neq 0, 1$

Quantity A	Quantity B
a^2	1

3. $3a + 5b = 12; \ 3b + 5a = 28$

Quantity A	Quantity B
$a + b$	5

4. A right circular cylinder of volume 200π cubic units has a height of 8.

Quantity A	Quantity B
The circumference of the cylinder's base	10

5. $x > 0$

Quantity A	Quantity B
The hypotenuse of a 45-45-90 triangle with a side of x	The longer side of a 30-60-90 triangle with a hypotenuse of x

6. $10 < \sqrt{x} < 14$

Quantity A	Quantity B
144	x

7. Rolling two standard six-sided dice

Quantity A	Quantity B
Odds of rolling a total of 6	Odds of rolling a total of 9

8. Sixteen ounces of lemonade mix makes two gallons of lemonade. (One gallon = four quarts.)

Quantity A	Quantity B
Amount of mix needed to make three quarts of lemonade	Six ounces of mix

Go on to next page

9. Bob traveled 40% of the distance of his trip alone, went another 20 miles with Anthony, and then finished the last half of the trip alone. How many miles long was the trip?

   Ⓐ 240

   Ⓑ 200

   Ⓒ 160

   Ⓓ 100

   Ⓔ 50

Questions 10—11 are based on the following graphs.

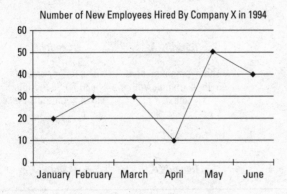

Number of New Employees Hired By Company X in 1994

Number of New Employees Laid Off By Company X

© John Wiley & Sons, Inc.

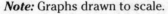

Note: Graphs drawn to scale.

10. If new employees hired in May 1994 were $\frac{1}{5}$ of the total employees, new employees laid off in 1994 would be what percent of the total employees in the company?

    Ⓐ 60

    Ⓑ 50

    Ⓒ $33\frac{1}{3}$

    Ⓓ 24

    Ⓔ 20

11. In 1995, the increase in the percentage of new employees laid off over that of the previous year was the same as the increase in the percentage of new employees hired between January and February of 1994. How many new employees were laid off in 1995?

    Ⓐ 10

    Ⓑ 20

    Ⓒ 50

    Ⓓ 60

    Ⓔ 75

12. Now in his second year at the firm, Carlos is earning an annual salary of $37,450. At the beginning of the year, he received a 7% raise. What was Carlos's starting salary?

    Give your answer to the nearest thousand.

    $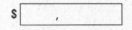

13. Jerry drives 30 miles per hour for two and a half hours. Susan goes the same distance but drives 40 miles per hour. How many hours does Susan drive?

    Ⓐ $37\frac{1}{2}$

    Ⓑ $1\frac{7}{8}$

    Ⓒ 2

    Ⓓ $1\frac{5}{8}$

    Ⓔ $2\frac{1}{2}$

Go on to next page ▶

14. Out of a class of 25 students, the teacher must choose 5 to represent the class in the school's spelling bee. Assuming the teacher chooses randomly, how many different combinations of students could possibly represent the class?

    Ⓐ 5

    Ⓑ $\dfrac{25!}{(25-5)!}$

    Ⓒ $\dfrac{25!}{5!}$

    Ⓓ $\dfrac{25!}{5!20!}$

    Ⓔ 1

15. Of 175 employees, 30 took advantage of prepaid legal services, 165 participated in the company retirement program, and 25 participated in both programs. How many employees did not participate in either program?

    Ⓐ 5

    Ⓑ 10

    Ⓒ 25

    Ⓓ 30

    Ⓔ 50

16. Common factors of 18 and 48 are

    Select all correct answers.

    Ⓐ 9

    Ⓑ 3

    Ⓒ 4

    Ⓓ 6

    Ⓔ 1

17. –5, 0, 5, –5, 0, 5, –5, 0, 5

    In the repeating sequence, what is the sum of the 250th and 251st terms?

    Ⓐ 5

    Ⓑ 10

    Ⓒ –5

    Ⓓ 0

    Ⓔ –10

18. How many ounces of 40% salt solution must be added to 75 ounces of 10% salt solution to make a 35% salt solution?

    Ⓐ 75

    Ⓑ 375

    Ⓒ 150

    Ⓓ 187.5

    Ⓔ 125

19. If $\dfrac{(x+5)}{(x-7)} = y$, what is the value of x in terms of y?

    Ⓐ $7y-5$

    Ⓑ $xy-7y-5$

    Ⓒ $\dfrac{(7y-5)}{(1-y)}$

    Ⓓ $\dfrac{-(7y+5)}{(1-y)}$

    Ⓔ $y-5+7$

20.

Company	Q1 Sales	Q2 Sales
A	$72,000	$80,000
B	$50,000	$59,000
C	$65,000	$73,000

© John Wiley & Sons, Inc.

Which of the following can be inferred from the data?

Select all that are correct.

Ⓐ Company B's increase in sales from Q1 to Q2 is greater than Company C's increase in sales from Q1 to Q2.

Ⓑ Company B's percentage increase from Q1 to Q2 is higher than that of either of the other two companies.

Ⓒ Company A's percentage increase in sales from Q1 to Q2 is greater than Company C's percentage increase in sales from Q1 to Q2.

STOP DO NOT TURN THE PAGE UNTIL TOLD TO DO SO. DO NOT RETURN TO A PREVIOUS TEST.

Chapter 7

Practice Exam 2: Answers and Explanations

A fter taking Practice Exam 2 in Chapter 6, use this chapter to check your answers and see how you did. Carefully review the explanations because doing so can help you understand why you missed the questions you did and also give you a better understanding of the thought process that helped you select the correct answers. If you're in a hurry, flip to the end of the chapter for an abbreviated answer key.

Analytical Writing Sections

Essay writing (and scoring) is subjective to some degree. There's no right or wrong answer, and every essay is slightly different. Evaluators, however, have a checklist of specific criteria for grading your essay. To check your own essay, consider the following questions:

- ✔ **Did you follow the instructions?** The prompt tells you what to do. For example, an Argument Analysis prompt may ask you to consider ways in which the argument relies on certain unstated assumptions, or it may instruct you to describe circumstances in which taking a certain course of action would or would not be best. To score well, you need to follow those instructions and write about what the prompt asks for.

- ✔ **Have you taken a clear stand in your essay?** Although arguing both sides of an issue or discussing strengths and weaknesses is fine, you must make your opinion or position clear. Don't expect the evaluators to infer your position. Be sure to *declare* your opinion in your introduction and be *consistent* throughout your essay.

- ✔ **Did you back up your stance with specific examples?** Anyone can state a position, but you must support your position with specific examples. You don't have to be right, but you do need to provide solid support for your claim. Also make sure your examples aren't easily refutable.

- ✔ **How quickly did you get to the point in each paragraph?** The evaluator will always look for your point in the first two lines of each paragraph, so don't try to be clever and write a paragraph with a surprise ending or twist. State clearly and unequivocally in the first line of each paragraph the point of that paragraph. Then spend the rest of the paragraph supporting that point.

- ✔ **Have you stayed on topic?** After stating your position in the introductory paragraph, make sure each succeeding paragraph supports that position instead of wandering off topic. Each paragraph should have a sentence (preferably at the end) that ties the paragraph directly to your position statement.

✔ **Did you avoid fluff?** Though longer essays typically earn higher scores, the higher scores are due to the fact that the essay provides sufficient support, not because it rambles on and on. Your essay won't be judged on word count; it will be judged on how sufficiently you explore the topic.

✔ **Does your essay maintain a professional tone?** The essay section isn't for creative writing. It's more like business writing, so avoid off-color language, slang, and inappropriate humor.

Section 1: Verbal Reasoning

1. **D.** *Ostensible* means apparent, outwardly appearing a certain way, which is the only answer that makes sense in the context of the second sentence. *Explicit*, *primary*, and *fundamental* all imply that the aim of the new bill was actually to cut spending. *Incipient* means something along the lines of saying that's how the bill started out, but it changed over time, which isn't supported in the context of the second sentence.

2. **A.** *Sophistry* is a word that describes an invalid argument that may seem *plausible* (believable) on its surface but is meant to be deceptive or misleading. *Dogmatism* is a strong assertion of opinions as truth, but the passage doesn't say that the administration merely laid down the law. *Bias* implies that the administration was predisposed not to support divestiture, which sort of works, but given the fact that the administration's intent was to deceive, *sophistry* is the better choice. *Probity* means integrity, honesty, and *glasnost* means transparency, both of which mean the opposite of what's called for here.

3. **B, D.** The account was too *elaborate* (detailed) and would have been more compelling had he *encapsulated* it (related only the most important parts). Neither *devious* (deceitful) nor *spurious* (false, fake) works with any of the words in the second column, because all those words relate to either making the story longer or shorter. If the story was too elaborate, then to improve it, the author would need to shorten it. *Expanded* and *embellished* both oppose the goal of making something shorter.

4. **C, F.** *Vitriol* means spiteful words, which you can't guess until you read the second sentence that mentions verbal battles. *Enmity* is a close second choice, but because the battles are verbal, *vitriol* is the better choice. *Pretense* means pretending to be something you're not.

   Aplomb is the ability to maintain composure, which makes sense in the context of the second sentence. *Effrontery* means boldness or audacity, which would make someone easier to draw into a heated debate. *Discomfiture* (*dis-* means not and *comfiture* means comfortable) means embarrassed or confused, which also doesn't convey the meaning of someone who's unlikely to engage in arguments.

5. **C, E.** *Viable* and *feasible* both describe an option or solution that can be implemented given the available resources. *Verifiable* means that something can be confirmed, which really doesn't fit with the rest of the sentence. *Standard* isn't even close. *Plausible* means believable, and *probable* means likely, neither of which applies to seeking solutions.

6. **B, F, I.** Reading this sentence the first time and filling in your own words, you may come up with something like, "Without *accurate* data to back up the researcher's claims, experts found the report's conclusions *questionable* at best and perhaps even *wrong*." *Empirical* evidence is derived from direct observation, making it the type of evidence experts would find more accurate. *Speculative* is abstract or unproven. *Scholarly* means educated, which doesn't fit as well as *empirical*. If the data were lacking, then the next two blanks would call for negative words. *Conceivable*, *convincing*, *certain*, and *ascertainable* fail to meet that condition. *Dubious* (doubtful) and *fraudulent* (falsified) convey the meaning that the data aren't to be trusted.

7. **A, F, G.** The key to choosing the correct words here is to read the passage in its entirety. If you do, you discover that the king's ultimate goal was to plant spies and other operatives

in the host country, which is not exactly a ***philanthropic*** (charitable) gesture. Knowing this, you can surmise that the king's plan was ***insidious*** (attractive on the surface but actually malicious), so what he was offering would seem to be ***magnanimous*** (generous). His true motive was to plant spies and other operatives, or ***infiltrate*** (get inside) the host country.

As for the other choices, for the first blank, ***innocuous*** means harmless, and ***vindictive*** means mean; although the king's plan may have been spiteful, *insidious* is the better choice because he offered something good and really had bad intentions. For the second blank, ***pedestrian*** means ordinary, which doesn't fit, and ***miserly*** means cheap, the opposite of *magnanimous*. For the third blank, ***inoculate*** means to prevent or protect, and ***obviate*** means to remove, neither of which fits the meaning of the sentence.

8. **D.** If nations use only waste products, edible portions of crops can still be used to feed people, so there's no need to stop production of biofuels immediately. If you picked Choice (A), that's certainly one argument, but non-food crops may require land that could be used to grow crop foods. Choice (B) may be true, but it doesn't undermine the argument. Choice (C) is fine if countries are concerned only about feeding their own citizens, but the discussion is global. Choice (E) may be true, but it doesn't undermine the argument.

9. **A, B.** To support Choice (A), the passage states that "the written words of foreigners are riddled with the cultural and social prejudices and misunderstandings characteristic of outsiders." To support Choice (B), the passage states, "Studies of archeology and language generally permit the historian to glimpse only very approximate timescales." Choice (C) is wrong, because the passage points out that although few societies in the precolonial past kept written records, the Arabic north was an exception. The statement "Historians have also had to make use of the written sources of foreigners, beginning with those of the Arabic-speaking travelers" further rules out Choice (C).

10. **D.** The passage reveals that historians have plenty of sources to draw from, but the sources vary in their accuracy and reliability. Due to the availability of resources, you can rule out Choice (A). You can also rule out Choice (B), because the passage indicates that recorded indigenous oral histories are available. Neither Choice (C) nor (E) is mentioned in the passage.

11. **D.** If students with lower scores drop out at significantly higher rates, this is a reflection of the students' ability: The students performed poorly not only on the test (with or without advance preparation) but also in coursework that the test preparation hadn't specifically prepared them for.

12. **B, C.** Senescent cells are in a "retirement-like state in which they die or no longer divide and thus become inert." Although the passage mentions the buildup of senescent cells in the cartilage, the passage doesn't cast this buildup as a characteristic of senescent cells.

13. **D.** "Though we casually consider the written and spoken forms of the word to be identical twins, they are really distant cousins." This is the only sentence in the passage that sums up its meaning.

14. **A.** According to the passage, "an actor may be able to express fifty different shades of feeling and meaning using tone, pitch, volume, accentuation, and facial and body gestures." The passage doesn't mention rhythm or resonance.

15. **B, E.** ***Pedantic*** and ***bombastic*** both describe someone who's pompous, which is exactly the kind of speech that would make someone seem ***pretentious*** (conceited). In one sense, ***austere*** (plain) means nearly the opposite; in another, it means serious or severe. ***Sonorous*** (loud, reverberating) could work if it had a match in the answer choices. ***Pusillanimous*** means cowardly or timid, and ***ravenous*** means really hungry.

16. **D, F.** ***Porous*** and ***permeable*** both mean full of holes, like a strainer or filter. A filter could be ***absorbent,*** too, but that would make it more like a sponge than a filter. If the filter were too ***resistant,*** nothing could pass through it. ***Dissolute*** means immoral, which would be more like unholy than holey, and ***dilatory*** means lazy or lagging behind.

17. **A, C.** *Exhaust* and *enervate* mean to weaken or wear out. Waves may *inflict* (impose something unwelcome) damage, but they don't inflict people. *Ameliorate* means to improve. To *castigate* is to scold or reprimand. *Energizing* is a trap, tempting you to choose two words that start with the same letters — *e-n-e-r*. However, *energize* and *enervate* have opposite meanings.

18. **B, F.** *Tendentious* and *partisan* mean biased. *Stubborn* also makes sense, but there's no match for it. *Independent* senators would not vote along party lines. *Insipid* senators would be dull. *Duplicitous* would work only if the senators promised to do one thing but did another.

19. **C, E.** *Venerate* means to worship, and one of the meanings of *aggrandize* is to glorify. You know from the second sentence that people in other countries are less impressed, so in the U.S., people must be more impressed. That means neither *disparage* (ridicule) nor *eschew* (reject) would work. For usage reasons, neither *embellish* (exaggerate) nor *proclaim* (announce) fits.

20. **D.** *Government spending* isn't mentioned in the passage. (Consumer spending is, but that's different.)

Section 2: Quantitative Reasoning

1. **B.** Suppose $a = 1$. Then Quantity A is $\left(\frac{1}{2}\right)^2 = \frac{1}{4}$. Quantity B requires you to square the 1 first, which is simply 1, giving you $\frac{1}{2}$. So far, Quantity B is bigger. Try a different number. Suppose $a = 2$. Then Quantity A is $\left(\frac{1}{4}\right)^2 = \frac{1}{16}$. Quantity B is $\frac{1}{2 \times 2^2} = \frac{1}{8}$, so Quantity B is still bigger. Apparently, the 2 is always squared in Quantity A but never in Quantity B. Quantity A thus always has a larger denominator, so Quantity B will always be greater.

2. **A.** Cancel values that are identical in both quantities, in this case the *a*, and you're left with *–c* and *+b*. Because *c* is negative, a negative *c* is positive. In Quantity B, *b* remains negative. Because any positive is greater than any negative, Quantity A is larger.

3. **B.** A 30-60-90 triangle has a side ratio of $side : side\sqrt{3} : 2side$. The side opposite the 30-degree angle is the shortest side — the 5 in this case. The side opposite the 60-degree angle is the next shortest side, the $side\sqrt{3}$ side. With this question, that's $5\sqrt{3}$. The area of a triangle is $\frac{1}{2}$base×height. The base is $5\sqrt{3}$, and the height is 5. Therefore, the area is $\frac{1}{2} \times 5\sqrt{3} \times 5 = \frac{25}{2}\sqrt{3}$. Don't bother finding the exact number — it's certainly less than $25\sqrt{3}$. If you thought the quantities were equal, you did *all* that work and fell for a different trap: forgetting to divide the *base* times *height* by 2.

4. **C.** Set up the equations vertically:

$$16a + 5b = 37$$
$$3b - 8a = -21$$

You want to either add or subtract the equations to get the same *numerical coefficient* (the number that goes in front of the variable) for the *a* and the *b*. When you add the equations here, you get $8a + 8b = 16$. Divide both sides by 8 to get $a + b = 2$.

5. **B.** Find the area of the square by squaring the side of 8, for an area of 64. Find the area of the circle by plugging the radius of 4, which is half the diameter of 8, into πr^2, for an area of 16π. Subtract the two for a leftover area (of the square not covered by the circle) of $64 - 16\pi$.

Don't bother figuring out how much 16π is. You know that π is slightly larger than 3. Multiply 16 by 3 to get 48. Subtract 48 from 64 to get a leftover area of 16. The actual leftover area will be even smaller, because 16π is more than 48. Because 16 is smaller than 20 and the *real* answer is even smaller than 16, Quantity B is bigger.

6. **B.** If square *RSTU* has a perimeter of 48, each side is 12. If the points are midpoints, each one divides the large square's sides into two parts, creating four isosceles right triangles (*RAD, SAB, TCB,* and *UDC*). The ratios of the sides of an isosceles right triangle are $side : side : side\sqrt{2}$. That means the hypotenuse of triangle *RAD,* for example, is $6\sqrt{2}$. These hypotenuses are the sides of square *ABCD*. Add the four sides to get $24\sqrt{2}$.

7. **C.** The key to this problem is knowing that Gigi and Neville work at the same rate. If they finish the lawn in 12 hours when working together, each did $\frac{1}{2}$ of the job in 12 hours. Therefore, Gigi working alone would've taken 24 hours to finish the lawn. Because 3 hours is $\frac{1}{8}$ of 24 hours, she could've done $\frac{1}{8}$ of the job in that time.

8. **5,000.** Latin American Sales account for 30% of total income. The equation is thus $\$50,000 = 0.3x$. Divide both sides through by 0.3 to get x (total income) $= \$166,667$. European sales were 20% of total income, or $\$166,667 \times 0.20 = \$33,333$. Sales to France were 15% of that figure: $\$33,333 \times 0.15 = \$4,999.95$. The answer needs to be to the nearest thousand, so round $\$4,999.95$ to $\$5,000$.

9. **E.** Read the titles of the graphs: They show income and sales from 1980 through 1990. The data doesn't show sales for one particular year.

10. **B, C.** Start with the first answer choice: Sales to Italy and Germany combined equal 40%. Sales to France equal 15%, which is not quite half as much, so cross the first choice off the list. The second choice is correct because sales to England and Italy are each 35%: $35\% - 15\% = 20\%$. The third choice is correct because $35\% - 15\% = 20\%$ and $15\% - 5\% = 10\%$. The last choice is wrong because half the sales to Italy is $35\% \div 2 = 17.5\%$, while sales to France is less than that at 15%.

11. **A.** The answers are in terms of x, so substitute $\frac{1}{x}$ for y in the equation:

$$\frac{1}{(x+1)} + \frac{1}{\left(\frac{1}{x}+1\right)}$$

Simplify the second fraction:

$$\frac{1}{\left(\frac{1}{x}+1\right)} = \frac{1}{\left(\frac{1}{x}+\frac{1}{1}\right)} = \frac{1}{\left(\frac{1+x}{x}\right)}$$

Dividing the 1 on top by the fraction below flips the fraction:

$$\frac{1}{\left(\frac{1+x}{x}\right)} = \frac{x}{(1+x)}$$

Now substitute $\frac{x}{(x+1)}$ for the second fraction in the original equation:

$$\frac{1}{(x+1)} + \frac{x}{(x+1)} = \frac{(x+1)}{(x+1)} = 1$$

12. **A, C.** Simplify and solve:

$$5(x+2)^2 - 125 = 0$$
$$5(x+2)^2 = 125$$
$$(x+2)^2 = 25$$
$$x+2 = \pm 5$$
$$x+2 = 5 \quad \text{or} \quad x+2 = -5$$
$$x = 3 \qquad\qquad x = -7$$

13. **A.** If ten plums cost a cents, then each plum costs $\frac{1}{10}a$ cents, and two plums cost $\frac{2}{10}a = \frac{1}{5}a$ cents. If six apples cost b cents, then each apple costs $\frac{1}{6}b$ cents, and two apples cost $\frac{2}{6}b = \frac{1}{3}b$ cents. Now, using 15 as a common denominator for 5 and 3, add the two costs:

$$\frac{3}{15}a + \frac{5}{15}b = \frac{3a}{15} + \frac{5b}{15} = \frac{3a+5b}{15}$$

14. **E.** The exponent −1 creates the reciprocal of that number. For the fraction $\frac{\sqrt{x}+2}{\sqrt{x}-2}$, the reciprocal is $\frac{\sqrt{x}-2}{\sqrt{x}+2}$, which is the answer.

15. **1:4.** First, back solve each circumference to find the radius of that cylinder:

Cylinder A   **Cylinder B**
$$2\pi r = 10\pi \qquad 2\pi r = 20\pi$$
$$r = 5 \qquad\qquad r = 10$$

Next, use $\pi r^2 h$ to find the volume of each cylinder:

Cylinder A   **Cylinder B**
$$V = \pi r^2 h \qquad\qquad V = \pi r^2 h$$
$$= \pi(5^2)10 \qquad\quad = \pi(10^2)10$$
$$= 250 \qquad\qquad\quad = 1{,}000$$

The ratio of the volume of Cylinder A to the volume of Cylinder B is 250:1,000, which reduces to 1:4.

A ratio is like a fraction — you can multiply or divide both sides by the same thing without changing its value. For example, 2:5 is equivalent to 4:10.

The GRE doesn't provide the formulas for the circle and the cylinder, so be sure to memorize them.

16. **B.** To find the average speed of a trip, place the total distance over the total time. You don't have the actual distance, but any number you pick will work, because the answer is in the form of a reduced fraction.

Pick a number for the distance. To simplify the math, use the lowest common multiple of the two speeds, 600 and 400, which is 1,200.

If the plane flew to New York, a distance of 1,200 miles, at 400 miles per hour, it flew for three hours. If it flew back at 600 miles per hour, it covered the 1,200 miles in two hours. Now you have the total distance and total time, which is 2,400 miles over five hours. Set up the average speed as a fraction, $\frac{2{,}400 \text{ mi}}{5 \text{ h}}$, and reduce to $\frac{480 \text{ mi}}{1 \text{ h}}$, or 480 mph.

17. **D.** Calculate slope with rise over run, or the formula $\frac{y_2 - y_1}{x_2 - x_1}$. Plug in the numbers and do the math:

$$\frac{14 - 2}{8 - 3} = \frac{12}{5}$$

18. **35.** The smallest prime number greater than 3 is 5, and the largest prime number less than 11 is 7, making a and b 5 and 7, respectively. Multiply these values for an answer of 35.

19. **A, D, E.** Because you're looking at the absolute value of x, the easiest way to answer this question is to ignore the negative signs in the answer choices, because the absolute value of a number is always its positive value. Drop the negative signs, and you immediately see that 21, 20, and 32 are all greater than 17.

20. **E.** Add the equations, and $4y$ and $-4y$ cancel out, leaving $16x = 48$, so $x = 3$. Plug 3 into either equation to find y: $9(3) - 4y = -5$, so $y = 8$. Therefore, x times y, which equals 3 times 8, is 24.

Section 3: Verbal Reasoning

1. **E.** An *imbroglio* is a complicated, embarrassing situation. A *coup* is an illegal overthrow of the government. As you may know (or deduce), *dissolution* is the process of dissolving or dissipating. A *caucus* is an assembly of political supporters. A *faux pas* (an embarrassing blunder) may trigger an imbroglio, but a release of documents wouldn't trigger a faux pas.

2. **B.** *Presumptuous* means to overstep boundaries, which intrusive advertising would be guilty of. *Abstemious* (restrained) means nearly the opposite. *Scurrilous* means vulgar, which may be a good second choice, but nothing in the passage suggests that push advertising contains vulgarity. *Pusillanimous* (timid) is another choice that's contrary to an intrusive practice. *Contumely* (treatment or language arising from contempt) certainly may be used in reference to inundating people with advertisements, but it's too strong for the overall meaning of the sentence.

3. **A, D.** *Dogmatic* means stubbornly narrow-minded and characterized by making assertions without backing them up with facts, which would explain why dictators are more skilled at enforcing policies than explaining them. *Intransigence* is stubbornness. As for the other choices, *acquiescent* (submissive) is the opposite of *dogmatic*. *Libertine* means morally unrestrained. *Diplomacy* involves mediation or negotiation, and *alacrity* is eagerness or enthusiasm.

4. **C, D.** *Plethora* means abundance, and if Alice was always at the top of her class, she must have had plenty of knowledge. *Paucity* means lack of, so if Alice had plenty of knowledge *but* a _____ of wisdom, she must have shown a lack of wisdom when trying to impress her friends. For the first blank, *scarcity* means the opposite of abundance, and *cache* is a collection of knowledge, which makes a good second choice. For the second blank, *surplus* is the opposite of lack of and *propensity* is a tendency to do something, which doesn't fit by usage or meaning.

5. **B, D.** *Vacillate* means to waver, so if the president vacillated on whether to approve funding, the contractors would be *wary* (cautious) about starting the project. *Vituperate* means to criticize harshly, which isn't an action you perform *on* something or to decide *whether* to do something. Also, the president may have *considered* whether to approve funding, but "considered on" doesn't work due to usage. In the second column, *weary* (tired) doesn't work and is included as a choice only to test whether you know the difference between wary and weary. *Perfidious* means deceitful, which isn't even close to making sense in this context.

6. **B, E, H.** To pick the right words for this sentence, start at the end. Knowing that the scholars were disappointed, you know that the first word must describe the review in negative terms. ***Banal*** (dull) is the only choice in the first column that fits. If the review was ***insightful*** (revealed deep understanding) or ***intriguing*** (compelling), scholars would have received it more positively. For the second blank, ***mandibular*** refers to the lower jaw, and ***secular*** means not religious, so ***conventional*** (predictable) is the only fitting choice. Finally, if the scholars were disappointed, they must have expected something better, ruling out ***tawdry*** (cheap, tasteless). They would want something more ***sophisticated*** (refined), not necessarily more ***prestigious*** (prominent).

7. **C, D, G.** Read the entire sentence, and you see it ends in sadness. It begins with the word *despite,* so you know it must begin on a lighter note. ***Levity*** (cheerfulness) is the only choice that meets that criterion; *seriousness* and *urgency* would call for something at the end that meant inaction. Because he remained _____ in the midst of cheerfulness, the second blank calls for a word like *sad*. ***Morose*** (deeply sad) is the best match; ***indifferent*** (uncaring) or ***unresponsive*** (insensitive) would pair up better with *seriousness* or *urgency* in the first drop-down list. Finally, you would expect the last word to mean something like tendency, and ***proclivity*** is the only word that fits. ***Appetite*** is similar in meaning, but you don't have an appetite *toward* something. ***Attitude*** suggests more of an opinion about something rather than a tendency toward.

8. **B.** If the flat tax didn't apply to capital gains and dividend income, which the most affluent citizens receive the most of, that wouldn't be fair. Choice (A) is wrong because the question specifically applies to taxpayers, not to those employed in the tax industry. Choice (C) supports the argument because those who can afford to pay more will. Choice (D) is wrong because it's about how much revenue will be collected, not about how payments will be evened out. As for Choice (E), even if a national sales tax were fairer, this doesn't mean a flat tax isn't fairer than the current system.

9. **A, B.** The passage states that current dietary staples make us fat and that the human genetic makeup has changed little since the Stone Age. Although the passage suggests that we eat foods similar to those eaten by hunters and gatherers, it doesn't suggest that we need to be hunters and gatherers.

10. **C.** Although the passage mentions that nature predisposed us to certain dietary needs, nothing in the passage suggests that the civilization of humans necessarily means that their diet gets worse.

11. **E.** Obviously, all the choices are supported in the passage, but read the question closely, and you know that the correct choice must be a sentence that sends a message to the reader. In this case, what is the author advising readers to do? The passage suggests that to remain healthy, humans must follow a diet similar to that of people in the Stone Age: "We need to give our bodies the foods we were originally designed to eat."

12. **B.** The passage describes Reynaud's method of drawing and painting directly on glass plates as "early works of animation." Standard photographs are mentioned but only in contrast to Man Ray's Rayographs. Projection is mentioned early in the passage but isn't described as a way of making a movie.

13. **B.** The first sentence begins, "Without any recording device whatever," indicating that the passage is about people who made films without using a camera to record video. Choice (A) is wrong, because the passage mentions the film *Mothlight,* released in 1963 (in the 20th century). Choice (C), *Beyond Filmmaking,* would make sense if the passage had discussed traditional filmmaking first and then proceeded to describe more advanced techniques. The passage does provide some support for Choice (D), *From Photographs to Moving Pictures,* but only one example in the passage mentions photographs. Choice (E), *Moth Wings and Other Snippets,* makes a compelling title but isn't the most descriptive.

14. **C.** All the answer choices are synonymous with ***audacious*** (bold), but ***intrepid*** (fearless) is the closest match. *Overconfident* is too strong a word, ***resolute*** means something more along the lines of following one's convictions, ***impudent*** is more like disrespectful, and ***pompous*** is more similar to arrogant.

15. **C, D.** *Extraneous* means unnecessary. *Superfluous* means more than what's needed. If the library received "so much" money, the county's contribution couldn't be *indispensible* (necessary) or *insufficient* (not enough). *Profligate* (wasteful) doesn't work, because it has no synonym in the list of answer choices. *Licentious* (immoral) isn't even in contention.

16. **A, D.** *Buttress* and *bolster* both mean to support or strengthen. If voters backed the candidate, they wouldn't *diminish* (lessen) or *undermine* (destroy) support. Neither *counterbalancing* (compensating for) nor *alleviating* (relieving) comes close to being correct.

17. **C, E.** An amusement park would want outgoing people to engage with patrons, so they would be looking for *gregarious* or *extroverted* (both of which mean *outgoing*) individuals. They wouldn't necessarily need to be *garrulous* (talkative) and certainly shouldn't be *diffident* (shy) or *introverted* (withdrawn). Being *benevolent* (kind) would be a plus, but it doesn't quite fit and has no match in the choices.

18. **B, F.** *Decorum* and *etiquette* both refer to the conventions of proper behavior. Someone who doesn't practice proper etiquette may be considered to be *boorish* (rude) or *decadent* (degenerate) or to be acting *disrespectfully,* so those words don't work. *Decoration* doesn't fit, because "rules of decoration" just doesn't sound right.

19. **A, F.** Because the judge found the suspect innocent, the prosecutor's reasoning must have seemed illogical or misleading. *Fallacious* may mean illogical or misleading, and *delusive* means misleading or deceptive. *Imperfect* (deficient) is a good second choice. *Legitimate* (valid) would probably lead to a guilty verdict. *Facetious* refers to saying something teasingly, not seriously. *Fallible* (susceptible to failure) would more accurately describe the prosecutor, not his reasoning.

20. **B.** Evidence of environmental damage from genetically engineered crops undermines the argument that these crops are good for the environment. Choice (A) states only that the benefits may be short-lived and suggests that long-term effects may prove to be detrimental. Choice (C) focuses more on the impact to humans. Choice (D) is too neutral to undermine the argument, and Choice (E) is more about protecting consumers than the environment.

Section 4: Quantitative Reasoning

1. **D.** The areas depend on how the figures are drawn. A rectangle of perimeter 20 can have, for example, sides of 1 and 9 and 1 and 9, making the area 9. Or it can have sides of 6 and 4 and 6 and 4, making the area 24. (The area of a rectangle is *length* times *width.*) A triangle of perimeter 20 can have sides of 5.5 and 5.5 with a base of 9, giving it a small area, or sides of 6 and 6 with a base of 7, giving it a large area. Either shape could have a greater area.

2. **D.** If a is a whole number, such as 2, then Quantity A is bigger. If a is a fraction, such as $\frac{1}{2}$, then $\left(\frac{1}{2}\right)^2 = \frac{1}{4}$ and Quantity B is bigger. Because you don't know what a is, the last choice is correct.

3. **C.** Line the equations up vertically and add them to get the same *numerical coefficients* (the numbers before the variables).

$$\begin{array}{r} (3a + 5b = 12) \\ +(5a + 3b = 28) \\ \hline 8a + 8b = 40 \end{array}$$

Now divide both sides of the equation by 8 to get $a + b = 5$, which means Quantity A equals Quantity B.

4. **A.** The volume of any 3-D figure on the GRE is *area of the base* times *height*. Because the base of a cylinder is a circle, the volume of a cylinder is $\pi r^2 h$. Divide the volume, 200π, by the height, 8, to find that the area of the base is 25π. Because the base is a circle of area πr^2, the radius is 5. But you're not finished yet.

   Circumference is $2\pi r$, which here is 10π. If you thought Quantities A and B were equal, you fell for the trap and forgot π, which is a common mistake.

5. **A.** Remember the common Pythagorean ratios. A 45-45-90 triangle has a side ratio of $x : x : x\sqrt{2}$, making Quantity A $x\sqrt{2}$. A 30-60-90 triangle has a side ratio of $x : 2x : x\sqrt{3}$, where $2x$ is the hypotenuse and $x\sqrt{3}$ is the longer side. Because the Quantity B triangle has a hypotenuse of x, divide the ratio in half, for $\frac{x}{2} : x : \frac{x\sqrt{3}}{2}$, making Quantity B equal $\frac{x\sqrt{3}}{2}$. Compare $x\sqrt{2}$ to $\frac{x\sqrt{3}}{2}$ by dropping the x's, giving $\sqrt{2}$ versus $\frac{\sqrt{3}}{2}$; therefore, Quantity A is larger.

6. **D.** If $\sqrt{x}$ is between 10 and 14, x must be a number between $10^2 = 100$ and $14^2 = 196$. Quantity A, 144, is also between 100 and 196, but without knowing the exact value of x, you don't have enough information to determine whether x is more or less than 144.

7. **A.** Write down the possible combinations for rolling each number, and you instantly see that the odds of rolling a total of 6 are greater:

   You can roll a 6 five different ways: 1 + 5, 2 + 4, 3 + 3, 5 + 1, and 4 + 2.

   You can roll a 9 four different ways: 3 + 6, 4 + 5, 5 + 4, and 6 + 3.

8. **C.** The GRE always gives you the units of conversion, except for units of time. Because a gallon is 4 quarts, 2 gallons is 8 quarts. If 16 ounces of mix make 8 quarts, then each quart requires $16 \div 8 = 2$ ounces of mix. To make 3 quarts, you'd need $3 \times 2 = 6$ ounces of mix, so Quantities A and B are equal.

9. **B.** If Bob traveled the last half of his trip alone, then the 40% and the 20 miles make up the first half, or 50%. Because $50\% - 40\% = 10\%$, 20 miles is 10%. Thinking in terms of fractions may be easier: $10\% = \frac{1}{10}$. If $\frac{1}{10}$ of *something* is 20, that *something* is 200. Arithmetically, you have $\frac{1}{10}x = 20$. Multiply both sides by 10 to get $x = 200$.

10. **E.** This problem takes two steps. The first chart shows 50 new employees were hired in May; therefore, $50 = \frac{1}{5} total$; solve for $total = (50)(5) = 250$ employees. Next, the second bar chart shows you 50 employees were laid off in 1994; therefore, $\frac{50 \text{ laid off}}{250 \text{ total}} = \frac{1}{5} = 20\%$.

11. **E.** First, figure out the percent increase in new hires between January and February. Twenty new employees were hired in January, and 30 were hired in February. To find a percent increase or decrease, you use the formula *number increase or decrease* divided by *original whole* (the number you began with). Here, that's $\frac{10}{20} = \frac{1}{2} = 50\%$.

   Looking at the second graph, you see that 50 new employees were laid off in 1994. Fifty percent of 50 is 25, so in 1995, $50 + 25 = 75$ new employees were laid off in 1995.

12. **35,000.** Because Carlos received a 7% raise, he now earns 107% of what he was earning initially. He's earning $37,500 now, so 107% of what he was earning is equal to $37,500. $107\% = 1.07$, so the equation looks like this: $1.07x = \$37,450$. To isolate the x, divide both sides by 1.07 for $35,000.

13. **B.** First, determine the distance Jerry drove: $30 \times 2.5 = 75$ miles. Because Susan drove the same distance, she drove 75 miles, too. Knowing her distance and that Susan drove 40 miles per hour, you now have everything you need to solve the problem:

$$40x = 75$$
$$x = \frac{\overset{15}{75}}{\underset{8}{40}}$$
$$x = 1\frac{7}{8}$$

14. **D.** This is a combination problem in which order doesn't matter, because to "choose 5" means students A, B, C, D, E are the same as students E, D, C, B, A . . . or any other mixture of these 5. Use the combination formula to solve the problem:

$$_nC_r = \frac{n!}{r!(n-r)!}$$

where C is the number of combinations you're trying to determine, n is the total number of objects or events (25 in this case), and r is the number of objects or events you're choosing at one time (5 in this case). You don't actually have to do the math — just set it up:

$$_{25}C_5 = \frac{25!}{5!(25-5)!} = \frac{25!}{5!20!}$$

15. **A.** To solve this problem, use this equation:

$$Group\ 1 + Group\ 2 + Neither\ Group - Both\ Groups = Total$$

Plug in the numbers and do the math:

$$30 + 165 + x - 25 = 175$$
$$x = 175 - 30 - 165 + 25$$
$$= 5$$

16. **B, D, E.** You could find all the common factors of 18 and 48, but instead, just try each answer choice. The first choice, 9, doesn't go into 48. The next choice, 3, goes into both 18 and 48. The third choice, 4, doesn't go into 18. The next choice, 6, goes into both 18 and 48. And the last choice, 1, is a factor of all integers, including 18 and 48.

17. **C.** The sequence has three terms (-5, 0, and 5), and every third term is 5. Divide 250 by 3 to get 83 with a remainder of 1. That means that the 249th number is 5 (because 249 divides evenly by 3); therefore, the 250th number is -5, and the 251st number is 0. Add to get $-5 + 0 = -5$.

18. **B.** Set up the equation with x as the number of ounces of 40% solution and $(75 + x)$ as the resulting number of ounces of 35% solution.

$$(75 \times 0.10) + 0.40x = 0.35(75 + x)$$
$$0.75 + 0.4x = 26.25 + 0.35x$$
$$0.4x - 0.35x = 26.25 - 0.75$$
$$0.05x = 25.5$$
$$x = 375$$

19. **D.** Multiply both sides by $(x - 7)$, and you get $x + 5 = xy - 7y$. Subtract 5 from both sides, and you get $x = xy - 7y - 5$. Now subtract xy from both sides to get $x - xy = -7y - 5$. You can factor the left side of the equation to get $x - xy = x(1 - y)$. Finally, divide both sides of the equation by $(1 - y)$, and you have your answer:

$$x = \frac{(-7y - 5)}{(1 - y)} = \frac{-(7y + 5)}{(1 - y)}$$

20. **A, B.** If you quickly scan the answer choices, you can see that they're all comparisons of either total sales or percentage increases, so you may as well figure out all the numbers before closely examining each choice:

Company A's increase in sales is $80,000 - $72,000 = $8,000$, representing a percentage increase of $\frac{\$8,000}{\$72,000} = 0.11 = 11\%$.

Company B's increase in sales is $59,000 - $50,000 = $9,000$, representing a percentage increase of $\frac{\$9,000}{\$50,000} = 0.18 = 18\%$.

Company C's increase in sales is $73,000 - $65,000 = $8,000$, representing a percentage increase of $\frac{\$8,000}{\$73,000} = 0.12 = 12\%$.

Answer Key for Practice Exam 2

Section 1: Verbal Reasoning	Section 2: Quantitative Reasoning	Section 3: Verbal Reasoning	Section 4: Quantitative Reasoning
1. D	1. B	1. E	1. D
2. A	2. A	2. B	2. D
3. B, D	3. B	3. A, D	3. C
4. C, F	4. C	4. C, D	4. A
5. C, E	5. B	5. B, D	5. A
6. B, F, I	6. B	6. B, E, H	6. D
7. A, F, G	7. C	7. C, D, G	7. A
8. D	8. **5,000**	8. B	8. C
9. A, B	9. E	9. A, B	9. B
10. D	10. B, C	10. C	10. E
11. D	11. A	11. E	11. E
12. B, C	12. A, C	12. B	12. **35,000**
13. D	13. A	13. B	13. B
14. A	14. E	14. C	14. D
15. B, E	15. **1:4**	15. C, D	15. A
16. D, F	16. B	16. A, D	16. B, D, E
17. A, C	17. D	17. C, E	17. C
18. B, F	18. **35**	18. B, F	18. B
19. C, E	19. A, D, E	19. A, F	19. D
20. D	20. E	20. B	20. A, B

Index

About the Authors

Ron Woldoff completed his dual master's degrees at Arizona State University and San Diego State University, where he studied the culmination of business and technology. After several years as a corporate consultant, Ron opened his own company, National Test Prep, where he helps students achieve their goals on the GMAT, GRE, and SAT. He created the programs and curricula for these tests from scratch, using his own observations of the tests and feedback from students. Ron has also taught his own GMAT and GRE programs as an adjunct instructor at both Northern Arizona University and the internationally acclaimed Thunderbird School of Global Management. Ron lives in Phoenix, Arizona, with his lovely wife, Leisah, and their three amazing boys, Zachary, Jadon, and Adam. You can find Ron on the web at testprepaz.com.

Joe Kraynak is a freelancer who specializes in team writing with professionals in various fields. He holds a BA in creative writing and philosophy and an MA in English literature from Purdue University and has coauthored numerous *For Dummies* titles, including *Bipolar Disorder For Dummies* with Candida Fink, MD; *Food Allergies For Dummies* with Robert A. Wood, MD; and *Flipping Houses For Dummies* with real-estate mogul Ralph R. Roberts. Joe lives in Crawfordsville, Indiana, with his wonderful wife, Cecie, three cats, and numerous forest critters. You can find Joe on the web at joekraynak.com.

Dedication

Ron Woldoff: This book is humbly dedicated to the many hundreds of students who have passed through my test-prep programs on their way to achieving their goals. You have taught me as much as I have taught you.

Authors' Acknowledgments

Ron Woldoff: I would like to thank my friend Elleyne Kase, who first connected me with the *For Dummies* folks and made this book happen. I would also like to thank my friends Ken Krueger, Lionel Hummel, and Jaime Abromovitz, who helped me get things started when I had this wild notion of helping people prepare for standardized college-admissions tests. And more than anyone else, I would like to thank my wife, Leisah, for her continuing support and for always being there for me.

Publisher's Acknowledgments

Acquisitions Editor: Erin Calligan Mooney

Development Editor: Victoria M. Adang

Copy Editor: Jennette ElNaggar

Technical Editor: Julie Dilday, senior editor with Langebartels Writing and Editing Services, LLC

Project Coordinator: Vinitha Vikraman

Cover Image: ©iStock.com/graphicsdunia4you

Apple & Mac

iPad For Dummies, 6th Edition
978-1-118-72306-7

iPhone For Dummies, 7th Edition
978-1-118-69083-3

Macs All-in-One For Dummies,
4th Edition
978-1-118-82210-4

OS X Mavericks For Dummies
978-1-118-69188-5

Blogging & Social Media

Facebook For Dummies, 5th Edition
978-1-118-63312-0

Social Media Engagement For Dummies
978-1-118-53019-1

WordPress For Dummies, 6th Edition
978-1-118-79161-5

Business

Stock Investing For Dummies,
4th Edition
978-1-118-37678-2

Investing For Dummies, 6th Edition
978-0-470-90545-6

Personal Finance For Dummies,
7th Edition
978-1-118-11785-9

QuickBooks 2014 For Dummies
978-1-118-72005-9

Small Business Marketing Kit
For Dummies, 3rd Edition
978-1-118-31183-7

Careers

Job Interviews For Dummies, 4th Edition
978-1-118-11290-8

Job Searching with Social Media
For Dummies, 2nd Edition
978-1-118-67856-5

Personal Branding For Dummies
978-1-118-11792-7

Resumes For Dummies, 6th Edition
978-0-470-87361-8

Starting an Etsy Business For Dummies,
2nd Edition
978-1-118-59024-9

Diet & Nutrition

Belly Fat Diet For Dummies
978-1-118-34585-6

Mediterranean Diet For Dummies
978-1-118-71525-3

Nutrition For Dummies, 5th Edition
978-0-470-93231-5

Digital Photography

Digital SLR Photography All-in-One
For Dummies, 2nd Edition
978-1-118-59082-9

Digital SLR Video & Filmmaking
For Dummies
978-1-118-36598-4

Photoshop Elements 12 For Dummies
978-1-118-72714-0

Gardening

Herb Gardening For Dummies,
2nd Edition
978-0-470-61778-6

Gardening with Free-Range Chickens
For Dummies
978-1-118-54754-0

Health

Boosting Your Immunity For Dummies
978-1-118-40200-9

Diabetes For Dummies, 4th Edition
978-1-118-29447-5

Living Paleo For Dummies
978-1-118-29405-5

Big Data

Big Data For Dummies
978-1-118-50422-2

Data Visualization For Dummies
978-1-118-50289-1

Hadoop For Dummies
978-1-118-60755-8

Language & Foreign Language

500 Spanish Verbs For Dummies
978-1-118-02382-2

English Grammar For Dummies,
2nd Edition
978-0-470-54664-2

French All-in-One For Dummies
978-1-118-22815-9

German Essentials For Dummies
978-1-118-18422-6

Italian For Dummies, 2nd Edition
978-1-118-00465-4

Math & Science

Algebra I For Dummies, 2nd Edition
978-0-470-55964-2

Available in print and e-book formats.

Available wherever books are sold. **For more information or to order direct visit www.dummies.com**

Anatomy and Physiology For Dummies,
2nd Edition
978-0-470-92326-9

Astronomy For Dummies, 3rd Edition
978-1-118-37697-3

Biology For Dummies, 2nd Edition
978-0-470-59875-7

Chemistry For Dummies, 2nd Edition
978-1-118-00730-3

1001 Algebra II Practice Problems
For Dummies
978-1-118-44662-1

Microsoft Office

Excel 2013 For Dummies
978-1-118-51012-4

Office 2013 All-in-One For Dummies
978-1-118-51636-2

PowerPoint 2013 For Dummies
978-1-118-50253-2

Word 2013 For Dummies
978-1-118-49123-2

Music

Blues Harmonica For Dummies
978-1-118-25269-7

Guitar For Dummies, 3rd Edition
978-1-118-11554-1

iPod & iTunes For Dummies, 10th Edition
978-1-118-50864-0

Programming

Beginning Programming with C
For Dummies
978-1-118-73763-7

Excel VBA Programming For Dummies,
3rd Edition
978-1-118-49037-2

Java For Dummies, 6th Edition
978-1-118-40780-6

Religion & Inspiration

The Bible For Dummies
978-0-7645-5296-0

Buddhism For Dummies, 2nd Edition
978-1-118-02379-2

Catholicism For Dummies, 2nd Edition
978-1-118-07778-8

Self-Help & Relationships

Beating Sugar Addiction For Dummies
978-1-118-54645-1

Meditation For Dummies, 3rd Edition
978-1-118-29144-3

Seniors

Laptops For Seniors For Dummies,
3rd Edition
978-1-118-71105-7

Computers For Seniors For Dummies,
3rd Edition
978-1-118-11553-4

iPad For Seniors For Dummies,
6th Edition
978-1-118-72826-0

Social Security For Dummies
978-1-118-20573-0

Smartphones & Tablets

Android Phones For Dummies,
2nd Edition
978-1-118-72030-1

Nexus Tablets For Dummies
978-1-118-77243-0

Samsung Galaxy S 4 For Dummies
978-1-118-64222-1

Samsung Galaxy Tabs For Dummies
978-1-118-77294-2

Test Prep

ACT For Dummies, 5th Edition
978-1-118-01259-8

ASVAB For Dummies, 3rd Edition
978-0-470-63760-9

GRE For Dummies, 7th Edition
978-0-470-88921-3

Officer Candidate Tests For Dummies
978-0-470-59876-4

Physician's Assistant Exam For Dummies
978-1-118-11556-5

Series 7 Exam For Dummies
978-0-470-09932-2

Windows 8

Windows 8.1 All-in-One For Dummies
978-1-118-82087-2

Windows 8.1 For Dummies
978-1-118-82121-3

Windows 8.1 For Dummies, Book + DVD
Bundle
978-1-118-82107-7

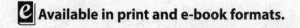 **Available in print and e-book formats.**

Available wherever books are sold. **For more information or to order direct visit www.dummies.com**

Take Dummies with you everywhere you go!

Whether you are excited about e-books, want more from the web, must have your mobile apps, or are swept up in social media, Dummies makes everything easier.

Leverage the Power

For Dummies is the global leader in the reference category and one of the most trusted and highly regarded brands in the world. No longer just focused on books, customers now have access to the For Dummies content they need in the format they want. Let us help you develop a solution that will fit your brand and help you connect with your customers.

Advertising & Sponsorships

Connect with an engaged audience on a powerful multimedia site, and position your message alongside expert how-to content.

Targeted ads • Video • Email marketing • Microsites • Sweepstakes sponsorship

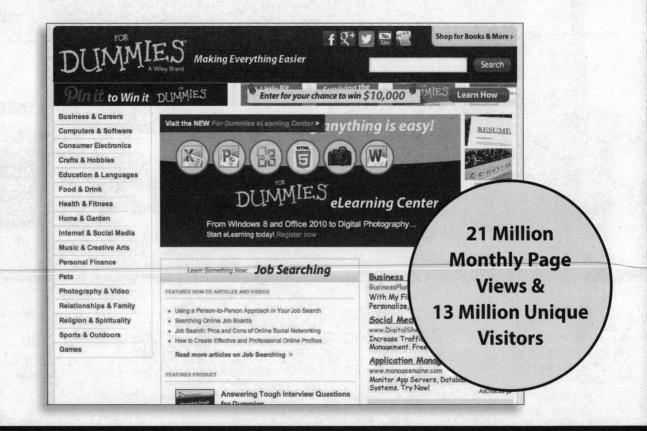

21 Million Monthly Page Views & 13 Million Unique Visitors

Custom Publishing

Reach a global audience in any language by creating a solution that will differentiate you from competitors, amplify your message, and encourage customers to make a buying decision.

Apps • Books • eBooks • Video • Audio • Webinars

Brand Licensing & Content

Leverage the strength of the world's most popular reference brand to reach new audiences and channels of distribution.

For more information, visit www.Dummies.com/biz

Dummies products make life easier!

- DIY
- Consumer Electronics
- Crafts

- Software
- Cookware
- Hobbies

- Videos
- Music
- Games
- and More!

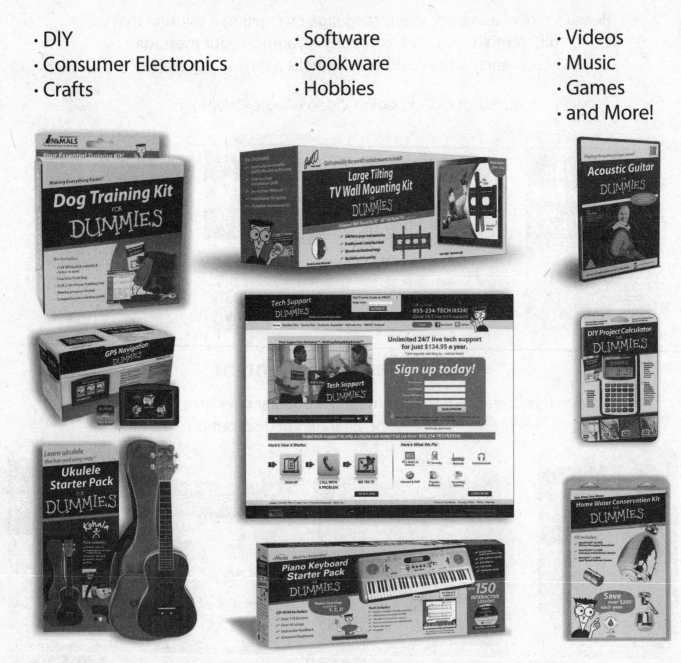

Dummies.com